MUSIC SUCCESS IN 9 WEEKS

A STEP-BY-STEP GUIDE TO SUPERCHARGE YOUR SOCIAL MEDIA & PR, BUILD YOUR FAN BASE, AND EARN MORE MONEY

3rd *edition*

by Ariel Hyatt
with *forward* by Derek Sivers

Music Success in 9 Weeks: A Step-By-Step Guide To Supercharge your Social Media & PR, Build your Fan Base, and Earn More Money, 3rd Edition.

Print edition ISBN # 978-0-9816331-4-5
Ebook ISBN # 978-0-9816331-5-2

Third edition, 2012.

Published by Ariel Publicity, Artist Relations, and Booking, LLC, 389 12th Street, Brooklyn, NY 11215.

Visit our website: *www.arielpublicity.com*
Email us: *contact@arielpublicity.com*

Third edition edited By Julia Rogers
www.juliarogers.com

Designed by Kristin Rogers Brown
www.kristinrogersbrowndesign.com

MASTERMIND FORUM

This book comes with lifetime membership and access to my closed, online Mastermind Forum for Extra Support.

On it you will be able to walk yourself through the steps in a group forum, get access to me and to my staff at Cyber PR®, and get valuable feedback.

Send an email to *Contact@ArielPublicity.com* to sign up, with the subject line "I bought the book!" You will receive a link for your account.

DEDICATION

To every single musician I have ever worked with.

You have given me your trust and your hard-earned money, and you have allowed me to help you with your art. Most of all, you have filled my life with the most joyful expression of humanity: Music.

Thank you for allowing me to live my dream.

It has been an honor and a pleasure to be of service.

ACKNOWLEDGEMENTS

To my mother—who blazed the trail...which is bright, wide-open, and ready for me to walk.

To my father—who makes me laugh every step of the way.

To Enid—for teaching me patience and for all of your love.

To Kristin Fayne-Mulroy—for your editing skills and your input, and for being my best friend since kindergarten.

To Derek Sivers—for constantly sharing your great ideas, and for being my sounding board in this amazing music business.

CONTENTS

FOREWORD BY DEREK SIVERS

It's easier than ever to be a musician these days.

You've got every tool you'll ever need. You can be your own label, distributor, agent, manager, publisher and promoter. Now is the ultimate time for DIY: You can do it ALL yourself.

It's harder than ever to be a musician these days.

Because you've got more tools than you'll ever need, nobody wants to help you anymore. They just point you to some advice and say, "Good luck." So, not only are you drowning in tools, but you're drowning in advice, too.

This situation is why Ariel Hyatt's *Music Success In 9 Weeks* book is what you need to get out of the dead end. For 20 years, Ariel's been a hands-on publicist for famous musicians. For 15 of these years, most independent musicians couldn't afford her hands-on service. But in this book, she shows you how to do exactly what she would do for you if you were paying her to work for you.

Instead of giving you a sea of disorganized advice, it presents very specific steps that say, "Do exactly this." Follow these steps, and your career will rise to a new level.

After you've risen above the clutter, you'll be surprised how many people are happy to help you.

—Derek Sivers, **founder, CD Baby,** *sivers.org*

INTRODUCTION

Congratulations.

You are taking a big step in your music career by purchasing this book.

I am excited to share this information with you. It is the culmination of my 18 years experience working in the music industry as a music publicist, observing and overseeing more than 1,700 PR and marketing campaigns, primarily for independent musicians.

Music Success in 9 Weeks *REALLY*?

Often when I speak at conferences and introduce this book, I am met with an inquisitive look: "So you really think you can make me have full success in just *9 weeks*?"

Some artists are downright insulted: "What are you talking about? I have already put in 8, 10 or 15 *years.* What is going to happen in 9 weeks?"

I'm not saying that your entire music career will be *made* (whatever that means these days).

What the title refers to is this: If you can separate yourself from your role as a musician (rehearsing, playing gigs, and writing songs) for 9 weeks and instead, wrap your head around marketing, fan engagement, and, yes, some self promotion, in 9 weeks you will see a marked difference in how your *business* looks.

When my friend and co-conspirator Derek Sivers, founder of *CD Baby*, helped me come up with the title of the book, we were trying to think of something that was digestible for artists and would give them a time frame by which they could take themselves out of the mindset of the creative process and put themselves into the mindset of the business process.

I strongly believe that true, gifted musical talent comes from within and can't be learned. It can be honed and tweaked, but not learned.

Luckily marketing, social media engagement, online promotion, and tactical marketing strategies CAN be learned. And that is what this book teaches, step by step.

By no means would I ever insult you by thinking that in 9 weeks I can transform all your music. But I'm pretty darn sure I can help you transform your marketing and promotion strategies and increase their effectiveness.

Builders vs. Idlers

Over the years I've noticed something that separates the artists I have represented into two categories.

The artists that are **Builders** experienced dramatic increases in their fan bases and saw palpable results as their careers grew. They have continued to consistently create more income and have gotten more exposure. I'm going to call these artists the **Builders** because their careers expand.

The artists in the second category have initially gained more PR exposure (because they've hired me to get them PR), so that has worked. But they have not seen a dramatic increase in their fan bases nor have their incomes increased. I call this group the **Idlers**.

The interesting thing is that the **Builders** are no better musically than the **Idlers**.

I can say, however, that the **Builders** I've worked with have always been more tenacious; they have never taken no for an answer, have never given up, and have worked harder and complained less than the **Idlers**. Because **Builders know** something that the **Idlers do not know**. I have outlined what they know and the actions they have taken, and I will explain how they have achieved more traction step by step in this book.

The steps outlined in this book are designed to turn you into a **Builder** and leave the **Idler** world behind.

By agreeing to become a student of the rapidly changing Internet—which is, in my humble opinion, the indisputable future of the music business—and by following this book's 9-week program, I promise that you will get results, because this system really works.

How do I know?

I have tested it with hundreds of my clients and with my own business. And when implemented, it has made and continues to make an impact.

Managing a boutique PR firm is a lot like managing an indie music career. Like you, I have events, a newsletter, and fans, and I also need to consistently develop a following in order to keep my agency going. Much like my artists, I work tirelessly to keep my dream alive.

The steps you are about to implement over the next 9 weeks have successfully increased my income and the incomes and fan bases of countless musicians I have worked with. They will also increase yours.

This 9-week course is a process that will take some time and effort to implement. And you may not actually be able to get it done in 9 weeks flat. Some of these steps may take you longer, and that's okay. I implore you to not get overwhelmed and feel as though you must do everything outlined here all at once. If you put one foot in front of the other, you will get results.

This book is packed with a lot of information, because there is a lot to learn as you go through this process. Each Week could be its own book. (In fact, I've written another book just about navigating Facebook and Twitter.) *Music Success in 9 Weeks* is an overview designed to get you on the court and give you a bird's eye view of the basics and how they all fit together into a cohesive system.

I think the reason social media specifically, but also all the other tools and processes in these book feel unimportant to most artists is because they can't see how they all fit together in a context. And that context is what *Music Success in 9 Weeks* aims to provide, so that each strategy will implore and inspire you to conquer it.

As Derek Sivers brilliantly advises, "Don't force yourself to do the things that you hate." So, I have ideas throughout to help you outsource and offload the things you really detest and don't want to do. But here's another observation I have made over the years: Artists who

have experience doing the things they don't enjoy—
tackling and completing them at least once—are able
to oversee these tasks much more effectively when the
time comes to let other people handle them.

That being said, if something I outline in the following chapters gives you that negative feeling in the pit of
your stomach, then outsource it to another member of
the band, your biggest fan, or your mom. But don't be
Sisyphus and try to push a boulder up the mountain.
(We all know what happened to him.)

Take this program one step at a time. You'll get the best
results if you read each step of the process and implement it in the order outlined in this book.

Here's to your success!

—*Ariel*

WEEK 1: SETTING GOALS

Before we dive into the full 9-week program of getting into action and learning, I want to help put you in the right frame of mind to tackle it all.

This step is supposed to be fun and creative. Do not look at this as an assignment; approach it as creatively as you can.

Make sure you have a notebook available where you can keep your thoughts and ideas. I suggest writing these exercises out by hand; however, if you take notes on a computer, create a separate folder so you can refer to them later.

Setting Goals

Starting this book with a clear set of goals is an empowering way to set the stage for your success.

Week 1 will assist you in creating a personal roadmap for achieving your goals in your musical career, whether music is your hobby or your full-time living.

Items you will need:

1. A blank notebook/diary/journal. (If you don't have one on hand right this moment it's OK; buy one ASAP.)
2. Several (10–12) pieces of blank paper.
3. Colored pens, crayons or watercolors.
4. An inspiring place—your studio, home, a coffee shop, etc.

An Astounding Fact—ONLY 3 PERCENT

Only 3 percent of all people have their long-term goals written down. And it has been proven that by simply writing down your goals, you are much more likely to achieve them.

I Repeat—Just By Completing This Exercise, You Are MUCH More Likely to Achieve Your Goals.

Dr. Edward Banfield of Harvard University concluded after more than 50 years of research that long-term perspective is the single most accurate predictor of upward social and economic mobility in America. It is more important than family background, education, race, intelligence, and connections in determining your success in life and work.

And it works!

Goal setting is the most powerful thing I have ever done for myself. Each year, I write down what I want to achieve for the year, both personally and for my business. Every month I write down what I have achieved, or check something off the list when I complete it. When you write out and measure your goals continuously, you will keep them present and alive on a daily basis. They will act as a roadmap and become your guiding beacons.

GOAL ACHIEVING TIP # 1: This is a Game; You Can Change the Rules as You Go

Goals are not written in stone and they are not the word of the Almighty. They should be looked at as beacons and guiding points to help keep you on track along your journey.

While I would not recommend changing your goals every week, the music industry is changing so rapidly, it's hard to know which goals are reachable in this landscape. So if in the course of the year your goals change, it's okay to cross one off, modify another, or start the game again and write new ones down as you go.

GOAL ACHIEVING TIP # 2: Don't Beat Yourself Up!

Implementing large, long-term goals may take a whole year (or more!), so be patient. You will have days where you may get frustrated, and you will start to beat yourself up. This is something I see a lot of my musicians do.

A client I represent will play an amazing set, get off-stage and all of a sudden start ripping into himself saying it sucked, or the sound was awful, or he couldn't hear himself, or he screwed up the entire second verse.

Sound familiar?

This kind of self criticism will interfere directly with achieving your goals and dreams.

So, the next time you are making yourself wrong, take a step back and try to take a moment to acknowledge the good, and take time to celebrate your wins.

GOAL ACHIEVING TIP # 3: 5 Successes Each Day

But, how do you "celebrate your wins"?

I'm inviting you to write down 5 little victories per day, not only for the coming 9 weeks, but also for an entire year, starting right now.

WRITTEN EXERCISE: YOUR 5 SUCCESSES

I learned this powerful technique from T. Harv Eker, author of *Secrets of the Millionaire Mind*.

He says that you should write down 5 little achievements every single day. Once you start getting into this habit, you are training yourself to put the focus on the positive and get your mind to stop being so self critical.

So put a notebook in your gig bag or next to your bed and throughout the next 9 weeks, write down 5 successes each day.

Make at least 1 or 2 of them music/music career related.

Here are some examples:

1. Went to gym.
2. Started writing lyrics to that song I've been thinking about.
3. Called 3 clubs for potential bookings.
4. Did laundry.
5. Reached out to a music blogger who will love my music.
6. Made dinner for my boyfriend/girlfriend/husband/wife/kids.
7. Added my band's profile on a social media site.

If you keep a journal or a notebook where you write lyrics, use that; if not, go purchase a blank book to write these in daily. It's amazing to look back over a year and read them all.

Your First 5 Successes

Right now, stop what you're doing and write down 5 tiny successes you had from today and yesterday.

1.

2.

3.

4.

5.

Day 2 Successes

1.

2.

3.

4.

5.

WRITTEN EXERCISE: GOAL SETTING

I suggest you write in pen using paper.

Your intention manifests differently when it comes from a pen and not from a computer. The act of writing accesses a different part of your brain and makes a deal between your hand, your mind, and your heart.

Write Down Your Focus Areas

Here is a list of some areas you may want to focus on. Skip the ones that are not for you and write out a goal in each area. Think big, be unreasonable, and don't hold yourself back.

Write Down At Least Six Focus Areas—Here Are A Few Ideas To Jump Start Your Brain:

» *Branding*—Creating a solid pitch and USP (Unique Selling Point).

» *Marketing*—What will you do this year for your marketing plan?

» *Online and social media strategies*—Do you have any, or any new additions to the ones you are already using?

» Does your website need a re-design?

» *PR* (getting covered on radio, online, TV, print media)—Have you written down where you see yourself reaching out for PR?

» *Booking*—What are your plans for touring or local gigs?

» *Music conferences*—Will you attend or play any?

» *Songwriting*—Are you writing songs? How many?

» *Albums*—Are you recording an album or an EP this year? In a studio or at home? How many tracks?

» *Sales*—How many CDs/downloads you would like to sell?

» *Money*—How much money you would like to earn?

» *Film and TV placements*—Will you focus on these?

» *Building your fan base*—How will you do this?

» *E-mail list*—How many people should be added?

» *Gig attendance*—How many people do you want at your next gig? How many people do you want at each gig for the next 12 months? (Write down an exact number.)

» *Team*—Will you focus on getting a manager/booking agent or publicist?

» *Your instrument*—Are you planning to buy a new instrument or sell your current one?.

» *Help*—Are you enlisting the help of your friends and family members?

» *Personal health* (to make your performance better)— Are you making changes to your exercise, nutrition and general health habits?

» *Mental health*—How will you stay in a positive frame of mind? Will you make time for meditation, time away, etc.?

Before You Get Started:
Techniques For Writing Down Goals

1. Be really clear about your goals—assign dates by when you will achieve each goal, and describe them in as much detail as you can.

2. Visualize and write each one as if it's already happening.

3. Your goals should involve you and only you (they can't be contingent on someone else).

4. Design goals so they are realistically achievable.

Write Out At Least 5 Goals Here:

1.

2.

3.

4.

5.

Getting Goals to Happen:

Do something every day that moves you towards achieving your goals. (Your list of 5 successes each day will help ground your frame of mind.)

Make daily lists of tasks you need to complete in order to get your goals met—the night before!

Write out a time frame for each task (15 minutes, 1 hour, etc.).

Do the hardest thing first in the morning; don't procrastinate.

Studies show that the average person can achieve 6 tasks a day so write a MAXIMUM of 6 per day so you don't get overwhelmed.

Delegate activities that waste your valuable time to other people. (You would be surprised what you could accomplish with the 4 hours it takes to clean your house.)

GOAL ACHIEVING TIP # 4: Build a Team

Build a TEAM to help you! Get an intern or two.

Log on to *http://www.entertainmentcareers.net* and post (for no charge) as an employer seeking interns. There are a lot of bright young people who would like to get their feet wet in the music business. You technically run a record label, so advertise for a label assistant, marketing manager or street team/social media director.

If you don't have an office to accommodate them that's okay; meet once a week at a coffee shop or have your intern work remotely from home as a virtual assistant.

GOAL ACHIEVING TIP # 5: Make One Happen ASAP

Start with the easiest goal on your list, give it a 2- to 4-week deadline, and then write out the goal in the present tense, as if it is already achieved, with a date, like this:

> *Today is [date], and I have added 25 new quality friends to my Facebook page.*

> *Today is [date], and I have created a Facebook fan page for my band, added music, and invited everyone to join it.*

Now, go back and put dates on every goal you wrote.

And here is the last part **of the exercise:**

Make the Goals Look Pretty & Hang Them Where You Can See Them Every Day

I highly recommend re-writing your goals neatly on paper. Use colored pens, watercolors, images from magazines, or crayons and illustrate them. Hang them in a place where you can see them every day. Remember, if your goals change, that's okay! Just cross one off and add a new one. You are the one in charge of your goals.

Suggestions:

Keep a few separate lists.

MUSIC **GOALS**—Next 12 months
MUSIC **GOALS**—In your lifetime
MONEY **GOALS**—Next 12 months
ANNUAL **GOALS**—For yourself/family
LIFETIME **GOALS**—What do you want in your whole life?

Remember to put the date by which you will achieve each goal.

Use the following pages or your own notebook.

MUSIC CAREER GOALS—Next 12 Months

DATE WRITTEN:

1.

By when:

DATE WRITTEN:

2.

By when:

DATE WRITTEN:

3.

By when:

DATE WRITTEN:

4.

By when:

DATE WRITTEN:

5.

By when:

MUSIC CAREER GOALS—In Your Lifetime

DATE WRITTEN:

1.

By when:

DATE WRITTEN:

2.

By when:

DATE WRITTEN:

3.

By when:

DATE WRITTEN:

4.

By when:

DATE WRITTEN:

5.

By when:

$ MONEY GOALS—Next 12 Months

DATE WRITTEN:

1.

By when:

....

DATE WRITTEN:

2.

By when:

....

DATE WRITTEN:

3.

By when:

....

DATE WRITTEN:

4.

By when:

....

DATE WRITTEN:

5.

By when:

....

LIFETIME GOALS + INTENTIONS

DATE WRITTEN:

1.

By when:

DATE WRITTEN:

2.

By when:

DATE WRITTEN:

3.

By when:

DATE WRITTEN:

4.

By when:

DATE WRITTEN:

5.

By when:

Can you come up with more?
Write them all! Think big!

NOTES

WEEK 2: THE PITCH

Creating The Perfect Pitch

This week is a key lesson in branding yourself, both online and offline. What you create here will define you in the minds of your fans and potential fans.

I encountered two scenarios that inspired the writing of this chapter:

Scenario #1:

I was out at the Mercury Lounge seeing a show, and between bands I was standing at the bar talking to some friends, when a musician handed me a show flyer. I was taken with him immediately; I always appreciate anyone who is self-promoting because it's not easy to do, and it's especially not easy to do at a crowded bar on a Wednesday night in downtown Manhattan.

I looked down at the flyer, and my heart sank. It said:

> Name of artist (not mentioned to protect the innocent)
> Venue (which was the Mercury, where I was)
> Time/date of show

There I was, a perfectly-primed potential fan, a customer standing at a bar, out at a live music show, and he lost me forever. Why?

Because not one sentence was included about the genre of music this artist played, much less what his music sounded like or who he was compared to (a sound-alike). In short I had no idea what to expect if I came out to his show.

To top it off, there was no website listed on the flyer. On the off chance that I had taken the flyer home, I would never have known where to listen to his music online.

That was a huge opportunity totally lost. Unbeknownst to him, he also handed his flyer to one of the most successful entertainment attorneys I know (who was in the middle of signing six artists to record deals), an A&R executive, and one of the best booking agents in the business.

We all looked down at the flyers in our hands, shrugged, put the flyers on the bar, and carried on with our conversation. He had totally blown it.

Scenario #2:

An artist called my PR firm to talk about hiring us for a Cyber PR® campaign, and two minutes into the conversation I was beginning to feel like he was totally wasting my time. It went something like this:

Me: "What do you sound like?"

Artist: "I sound like absolutely nothing you've ever heard before."

Me: (annoyed and understanding why he's not where he wants to be as an artist) "Really? So you've invented a new genre of music, and you don't sound like anyone else in the history of music?"

Artist: "Yes."

Me: "Can you at least tell me what type of music you play?"

Artist: "It's old-school hip hop."

OK, finally we were getting somewhere. Now, while I totally understood his point, here's the problem with having an approach like his:

People are constantly looking for a *context* to put things into. And if you don't provide them with one, they will move on to the next thing that their little pea brains can actually grasp.

The critical thing that was missing in both scenarios was The Pitch.

A pitch is sometimes called your Elevator Pitch (how you can describe yourself in the course of an elevator ride); marketers call it a USP (Unique Selling Point); my friend Bob Baker calls it a BIS (Brand Identity Statement). And Laura Allen, founder of 15secondpitch.com, has trimmed it down to a 15-second pitch!

Call it what you want, this thing will change the way you market yourself and your music and give everyone some context to understand what you do. It is critical that you have a concise and easy-to-understand pitch that will help you shape your brand.

Your pitch does not have to be lengthy to be effective; it just has to explain your sound in a few words or sentences.

Here are some of my clients' best pitches to jump-start your brain:

The Divorcees—The hard liquor sandwich of Americana: 1 shot each of Jager (Cash), Tequila (Willie) and Whiskey (Waylon)

Leftover Salmon—Polyethnic Cajun Slamgrass

John Taglieri—If Vertical Horizon and Third Eye Blind got hit by Train!

Devil Doll—Jessica Rabbit meets Joan Jett

Kara Aubrey—Mad Moxie Rock; Pat Benatar, Pink, and Paramore.

Movie Time

Here are some videos of me talking with two experts about how to craft the perfect pitch.

» Ariel Hyatt & Derek Sivers discuss the pitch, Part 1—"Why It's Critical to Have a Pitch" *http://bit.ly/DerekArielPitch1*

» Ariel Hyatt & Derek Sivers discuss the pitch, Part 2—"Hillbilly Flamenco: Finding 2 Great Words that Changed a Band's Entire Path" *http://bit.ly/DerekArielPitch2*

» Ariel Hyatt & Laura Allen of *15SecondPitch.com* discuss why a pitch is needed and how to hone the perfect one in a simple 4-step process. *http://bit.ly/LauraArielPitch1*

» Ariel Hyatt & Laura Allen of 15SecondPitch.com discuss where your pitch should be placed after you create it. *http://bit.ly/LauraArielPitch2*

CREATING YOUR PITCH

First, take a deep breath, clear your head, and keep in mind that what you are about to do is a lot like writing song lyrics.

You don't record the first thing that comes out (or at least I hope you don't. But that's a different conversation). It takes some honing, some tweaking and possibly some collaboration. And so does crafting your pitch.

STEP 1: Write Down the Details

1. Genres you play: Roots, rock, reggae, folk, punk, jazz, alt-country, chillout, funk, etc. (No more than two or three will actually be selected in the end.)

2. All the artists that other people say you sound like.

3. All artists (or authors, or famous people, or places, or things) that have influenced you.

4. All the feelings and vibes you want to create or convey with your music.

STEP 2: Choose Your Favorites

Now look back at your notes and use these elements as a guideline to help you come up with a few words or sentences that sum you up.

Circle the ones that resonate the most with you.

STEP 3: Log On And Test It Out

Go to this fabulous website:

http://www.15secondpitch.com

This website will help you structure and hone your pitch. And it will TIME you, too!

(This site is a business pitch site. But you ARE a business and the structure that it provides is very helpful.)

STEP 4: Write Out Your Pitch

Do you love it?

If you don't, then don't use it.

I once worked with a band that chose the term "Soul Rock" to describe their sound. After it was published countless times they were hating it. Make sure your pitch is something that you will like when you hear it over and over again and that it's something you won't get sick of.

STEP 5: Say It Loud

Now stand in front of the mirror and practice saying it out loud.

Does it feel comfortable to say it?

If you feel like you're speaking your truth, you will absolutely know. And then, it is the perfect pitch for you.

Still not sure? Read it to a bunch of friends and fans and ask them to work on it with you. Don't over-think it. Keep it as simple and as concise as you can.

STEP 6: Place Your Pitch

Now that you have it, you're going to place it in the following places.

What you are doing now is branding yourself.

Online Branding:

Place your pitch...

1. On your website's homepage (yes, on the HOMEPAGE, and on as many pages as you can: at the top of your bio and on any page your fans may land, not buried in the site).

2. On your Facebook fan page—in the area that says "info."

3. On your Twitter page—in the area that says "bio." (Don't forget the link to your site.)

4. On your Myspace page (yep, still).

5. On all other social networking sites and anywhere else you have an online presence.

Offline Branding:

Place your pitch...

1. On your postcards.
2. On your show flyers.
3. On your business cards.
4. On your posters.
5. On anything else you have in print.

So now when you're out somewhere and you hand someone a flyer announcing your show, you're handing someone your brand.

People will know exactly what you do, and it will be truly effective marketing.

Not sure if you've hit the nail on the head?

FREE PITCH ANALYSIS—FROM TEAM CYBER PR®

This book comes with a membership to my private on-line Mastermind Group.

To join the Mastermind Group send an e-mail that says "I bought Music Success in 9 Weeks" to: Contact@ArielPublicity.com

NOTES

WEEK 3: YOUR WEBSITE

I've seen it time and time again: A creative mind will sabotage an effective website. Your website should be an expression of you and your music. However, there is a science behind what makes an effective website that way too many people ignore because they confuse "website" with "art".

Your website exists to do 3 things:

1. Clearly explain the basics about you (Who, What, When, Where, Why, How).
2. Help you capture and engage fans.
3. Make you $$$.

I have spoken in over a dozen countries to literally hundreds of artists who are experiencing the same problems:

1. Their website is out of their control. (It's being run by a web designer who charges too much or is not readily available, and he is the only person who can update it.)

2. Their website is outdated/antiquated.

If you have not spent any time fixing these problems, the time is NOW. Your website is your home base and your very own shingle that hangs online for the entire world to see. You need to make sure you are in control of it.

Here are my website basic tips. Included are some affordable solutions to pay as you go; there is no longer an excuse for not having an updated site that you control.

Here's how to set yourself on the right path.

THE MUSICIAN'S GUIDE TO AFFORDABLE, EFFECTIVE WEBSITES

STEP 1: Register Your Domain.

Every website has a domain and you must pay to register a domain name. To register a domain name go to *godaddy.com* (USA) or *crazydomains.com.au* (AUS).

Register the domain that you would like to use. I highly suggest a dot com (.com) if you can get one and no slashes or underscores if you can help it.

TIP: You should also make sure that the YouTube, Twitter, and Facebook page names are available. Ideally, all your socials should match.

STEP 2: Choose How You Would Like to Build Your Site.

Option #1: Pay as You Go & Build it Yourself.

A pay-as-you-go option with a web site builder can get you up and running very quickly, and you won't need a designer to build for you. Here are my favorite 4 in alphabetical order. All 4 have excellent call-in customer service to help ease the confusion.

» **Bandzoogle**—*http://bandzoogle.com*: Their "lite" version starts at $9.95 per month. It's easy to use, and the first month is free!

» **Hostbaby**—*http://www.hostbaby.com*: Owned by CD Baby, Hostbaby has recently undergone a fabulous face-lift and is easy to use. You can store unlimited e-mails and send newsletters through your custom site. It costs $20 per month, or $199 per year.

» **Nimbit**—*http://www.nimbit.com/instant-band-site*: You'll need a Nimbit account (either Free, Indie, or NimbitPro—all the details are on the site). Note: these are real Wordpress sites! If you want a Wordpress site, this is a great pay-as-you-go option. It offers easy tutorials, too!

» **Onesheet**—*http://www.onesheet.com*: There is a new fabulous site builder in town brought to us from the wonderful Brenden Mulligan, who founded ArtistData.com and sold it to Sonicbids. Onesheet allows you to build a slick website that incorporates all the necessities outlined in this chapter. At the time this book was published it is the newest player on the scene. And I think it just may be the best and easiest solution for musicians available.

TIP: Create a Onesheet and forward your *domain.com* to it, and, Voilia—a fabulous and integrated Website for free!

Option #2: Work With a Web Designer.

Gone are the days of hiring expensive web designers. I do not believe you need them. I love Wordpress, which is an open platform that will deliver a clean, beautiful website that you can update and control. The learning curve is not that steep, and once you master the back-end editing you can update your site from anywhere.

If you do not know any web designers who can build a site using Wordpress, I suggest using crowdspring.com. This is a site where designers bid against each other to work with you. I like it because crowdspring holds your money in escrow until you are satisfied with the designer's work, which means there is no way you can lose your money to someone you don't trust. Make sure you read the designers' reviews and see examples of his work before you hire him so you don't get any surprises.

TIP: Don't pay more than $500 for a basic Wordpress site.

TIP: Don't work with an "arty" web designer who does not build in Wordpress, because he will likely give you a flash movie intro or a complicated site. If you want "arty," buy a fabulous new outfit, or create a physical piece of merchandise that is cool and expresses who you are. But please don't be "arty" on your website; be clear and functional.

EFFECTIVE WEBSITE DESIGN GUIDE

Make Sure Your Brand is Consistent Throughout Your Site.

Brand your site with your look, your colors, and your logo (if you have a logo)...and of course, choose a stunning photo of you/your band.

TIP: Your social media sites (Facebook, Twitter, You-Tube, etc.) should match your site colors.

Components of Your Landing Page/Homepage

Navigation Bar

Your homepage should be easy to navigate with a navigation bar across the very top or down the left hand side (at the top) so visitors can see it. Don't bury information or make visitors scroll down to see it.

Pitch

Your homepage should feature your name, your pitch, or specifically what you sound like in a few words. If you feel weird creating a "pitch" on your own, you can also turn one killer press quote or fan quote, which sums up the way you sound into an effective pitch. (Refer back to *Week 2* of this book for more help crafting your perfect pitch!)

Irresistible Offer

Make sure your site features a FREE, exclusive MP3, video, or special white paper in exchange for an e-mail address.

The following sites have great widgets your designer can easily install:

Reverbnation—*http://bit.ly/reverbfreebribe*
Pledgemusic—*http://bit.ly/pledgefreebribe*
Topspin—*http://www.topspinmedia.com*
Noisetrade—*http://www.noisetrade.com*

Link Your Social Media Sites & Blog.

Your homepage should include links to your Facebook, Twitter, Google+, YouTube, Myspace, Reverbnation, Sonicbids, Last.fm and anywhere else you maintain an active profile.

» Include a Facebook "like" widget.

» Include a Twitter stream updating in real time with a call to action that says, "Follow Me." (The word "follow" actually makes people take action.)

» Make sure you have a blog feed / news feed, or new shows updating onto the page.

» If you like sharing photos, include a Flickr stream, which your designer can set up to port over to your blog.

Navigation Bar Elements / Tabs:

Here are the tabs that should go under the navigation bar:

1. **Bio/ Press Kit.** For your press kits, use Sonic Bids or Reverbnation.

   TIP: (for photos/ images) Make sure your photos really capture who you are and include clear instructions for how they can be downloaded. Include lo-res (thumbnail) and hi-res versions.

2. **Buy Music—iTunes, CD Baby or another storefront.**

3. **Tour Dates**—Dates of tours and any other shows or performances.

4. **Your Blog**—Link to it and update at least two times per month.

5. **Your Contact Info**—Make sure you have your contact information with an e-mail address or a contact form there so people can contact you for online publicity, booking, or just to tell you they like your music.

TIP: Don't ever make it hard for anyone to find you online.

TIP: After your site is built make sure to keep your social media sites updated...daily. This way your whole site remains interesting, dynamic, and fully updated.

As is the case with all forms of social media, your website is all about two-way conversations—not just about having a static website packed with unchanging brochure-like material. You want an interactive and engaging website that pulls people in at first and makes them want to come back often and interact with you.

6 SURE-FIRE WAYS TO CATCH & HOLD YOUR FAN BASE

Follow these rules and start getting casual visitors to become engaged fans.

1. Add Your Pitch to Your Homepage.

Last week you created your pitch and by now you should have already added it to your homepage and anywhere else you have an online presence: Twitter; Facebook; YouTube; Myspace.

If you have not done this already, please go back and handle this important step before you move ahead with *Week 3.*

2. Your Site Must Load in less than 3.5 Seconds.

All studies show that people have the attention span of gnats and that if they have to wait more than 3.5 seconds for a site to load, they'll move on to another site. So, time your site and make sure it loads in less than 3.5 seconds.

3. Avoid Flash Intros.

Flash intros are becoming less and less popular. If you still have one, I urge you to resist the temptation to keep it! You want to have a clean, easy-to-load page that instantly connects you and your information directly to your fans. Previously, Flash intros were unreadable to search engines, meaning you would not be findable in Google, which is critical to your online strategy and your online success. The newest versions of Flash actually are readable by search engines. But I still suggest you skip it altogether.

4. Have a Consistent Look, Feel, and Name All Over the Net.

Your site should have the same color scheme and theme throughout ALL the pages so that visitors do not think they have landed on another site while surfing through yours. Studies show that when people feel uncomfortable online they move on—and they feel uncomfortable when the consistency changes. The same goes for social networking sites; make sure your Facebook, YouTube, and Twitter themes match your website. If your website is blue, your Facebook, YouTube, and Twitter pages should also be blue. Also, use the same username wherever possible: You.com should match your Facebook.com/you and your Twitter/you.

5. Give Away an Exclusive, Free MP3 / Video to Satisfy the WIIFM—"What's In It For Me?" (your fan's little voice)

Every consumer (read "fan") on earth, when confronted with the option to buy something or simply take action is thinking: "WIIFM?" or "What's In It For Me?" The "What's in it for me?" question is driving your fans at all times. Therefore, you must offer them something they can't refuse.

People can't refuse unique and special offerings that are free; so offer free MP3s or videos on your website! Use this irresistible offer to encourage people to sign up for your e-mail list, which should be prominently featured on your homepage.

TIP: Make sure the offer is exclusive only to your website and *not* available anywhere else online.

This irresistible offer is a gift that people receive when they sign up for your monthly newsletter; it's your way of saying, "Thank you for being my fan!"

DO NOT put a box on your page saying, "Join Our E-mail List." What this is conveying is, "Hey fan sign up for our e-mail list so we can send you *more* e-mail." Instead, make an offer they can't refuse. Word it in a way that answers the WIIFM question. I recommend saying, "Sign Up For Our Monthly Newsletter List and Receive Exclusive MP3s Every Single Month," or "Sign Up For Our Mailing List and Receive a Free Download Instantly."

TIP: Your webmaster should be able to program this easily using widgets. If you don't have a webmaster that can handle this, I suggest the ReverbNation widget called "Exclusive Downloads." You can find it at the following link: *http://bit.ly/reverbfreebribe*. To install it on your Facebook fan page, just follow directions on the ReverbNation site.

6. Make It Clear, and Set Them at Ease.

You want to make sure it is very obvious to your visitors that the moment they sign up on your mailing list they will be receiving their free MP3 or video, and that they're also getting signed up for your newsletter.

Also, on your homepage, you should put in small letters:

"We will never sell, rent or lend your e-mail addresses to anyone else ever," so that people can be assured that their e-mail addresses are safe with you. Here are 3 more examples of statements you can make to convey this message:

1. "We will never rent, sell or share our subscriber list. Period."

2. "We love you and respect your privacy. And we won't ever sell, rent or loan any of your contact information to any third parties."

3. "Your e-mail address is safe with us. We will never sell, rent or loan it or any information you provide us to anyone, no matter what."

TIP: It is NOT COOL (actually it may be illegal) to sign people up to your e-mail list without their permission, so make sure you ask if it's OK before you sign anyone up to receive your newsletter, as you do not want to be reported as a spammer.

OPTIMIZING YOUR WEBSITE

How to Post a Perfect Press Kit on Your Website

I am amazed how hard it can be to find simple press components on many artists' websites. Here are 3 critical components that you should include on the press page of your website. These components show music writers and calendar editors that you care about making their lives easier. Editors need access to your information quickly, because they are constantly under a deadline. If you do not make it easy for them to get your information from your site, they may move onto another one of the 50 artists that are playing their market that same week.

1. Your Music—Album or Live Tracks

Make sure you have some music available on your website or a very obvious link to your Facebook where people can hear the music instantly. Many newspapers are now including MP3s of artists coming to town in the online versions of their papers, so make it easy for them to download the tracks to add to their own sites; this is additional excellent exposure for you.

2. Biography—Must Include Your Pitch

Make sure you have a short, succinct bio that can be easily located on your site in addition to the long-form bio. I suggest having three bios:

1. Long form
2. 50 words or less
3. 10 words (a tweet)

Make sure this bio can be easily cut and pasted so writers can drop it into a preview or a column. Also include a short summary (less than 10 words)—your pitch—that sums up your sound for calendar editors.

You can also include the blogs and all the opinions from each band member. But remember that while these extras are fun for your fans, they are not necessarily useful for music writers who will be looking to get quick information.

TIP: Do NOT have your bio in Flash format, so cutting and pasting right off your site is easy for editors.

3. Photos—Make Them Easy to Find and Download

Thumbnails are great for quick and easy loading, but are detrimental for use in newspapers. You should always have a few downloadable photos on your site in at least 300 dpi/jpg format.

TIP: Create an easy-to-see link that says "click here for a hi-res jpg." That way photo editors can get to them easily. When the photos are downloaded, make sure they are properly named with your name or your band's name, so that photo editors can find them in folders.

TIP: Remember to change your photos a few times a year, so if you play the same markets over and over, you can give the media multiple options for covering you.

TIP: Put the band members' names from left to right (L-R) under the band photo to give journalists a point of reference. Many publications publish photos with all band members' names from left to right to save the writers the trouble of having to ask for the names.

4. Include Your Album Cover Artwork

You also want to make sure you include your cover art in both hi-res and lo-res (jpg) format. This way if your CD is being reviewed, the writer can download the artwork.

What the Heck is SEO/SEM?

You may have heard the terms "SEO" or "SEM" and wondered what they mean. In plain English, Search Engine Optimization (SEO) or Search Engine Marketing (SEM) both refer to the process of improving the visibility of a website in Google (and other search engines). A site that is higher up on the page and appears more often in the search results list will get the most visitors. SEO can target different types of "search," including image search, local search, video search and news search.

Creating a great deal of content related to your band's name, mission, and music can serve you well with SEO/SEM and therefore really build your brand. But optimizing your website is not just about plastering your band name all over your website. While you might appear at the top of the list in search results for your specific band name today, you never know what might be happening elsewhere on the web that might possibly dislodge you from that top spot.

For example, a negative review or a blog comment that is unflattering about you could get posted on a high-ranking blog or music site and that could become the #1 search result in Google. It happens all the time.

Owning your own name as a domain name is the biggest part of securing your rank in searches for your name. But there are other components that are also very important—like Title and Meta Tags, default tags, and how frequently you update your website content, etc.— not only for your band name, but also for the keywords that you choose to define yourself online. Any good web designer will know how to manage keywords. But it's important for you to understand the basics.

It's not necessary to know about SEO/SEM in depth if you are just starting out. But these terms will crop up, and I did not want to leave you in the dark.

Definition: Meta Tag

A special HTML tag that provides information about a web page. Unlike normal HTML tags, meta tags do not affect how the page is displayed. Instead, they provide information such as who created the page, how often it is updated, what the page is about, and which keywords represent the page's content. Many search engines use this information when building their indices.

Definition: Title Tag

An HTML title element that is used to briefly and accurately describe the topic and theme of a web page and is important to both SEO and the user experience. It displays in two key places: the top bar of internet browsers; in search results. When search engines used simpler algorithms, the title tag was the single most important on-page SEO factor. Now it acts as an easy way to determine the topic and relevancy of a page.

ADDITIONAL TOOLS TO HELP YOU BUILD AND OPTIMIZE YOUR OWN WEBSITE

More About Working with Wordpress

Wordpress is an open source blog tool and publishing platform and can be used to build your entire website, so you need not bother with a web designer once the foundation of the site is built. If you get help setting up your website, be sure to ask for full administrator rights so you can easily update and change content. Wordpress also offers hosting for any site.

Some Tips for Using Wordpress

When you use Wordpress, the following suggestions will help you get the most out of your experience:

» Install the all-in-one SEO plug-in. This will allow you to easily input Meta and title tags for each post and page.

» There are also plugins that allow you to easily install Google Analytics and Google XML site map for better search engine results. Under plugins hit "add new" and search for both terms to get a list of options.

Definition: Plugin

A software component that adds to the functionality of your Wordpress website. This component "plugs into" the application.

NOTE: Always make sure that the plugins you select are tested to be compatible with the version of Wordpress you're using.

» Tag and use categories for every post and page. It may seem like overkill, but it will really help ensure people stumble across your site, especially if you are blogging a lot.

» Use "pretty linking." This just means that you make sure the URL of each blog post includes the category and title of that post. This will improve your chances of people finding your site through search engines. (And you want to jump on ANY strategy that might draw people to your site!) Wordpress makes this process easy by offering an editable URL field, so you can create a URL in the same area as you create your blog post.

Measuring the Effectiveness of Your Website with Google Analytics (GA)

TIP: If this seems confusing or overwhelming, any web designer can install Google Analytics for you.

Adding HTML Code to Your Website Template

There is a more permanent and slightly more involved way to add the analytics code to your site. The code can be added into the template itself. The way Wordpress templates work, there is usually a file called footer.php which controls the content displayed at the bottom of each page.

While the placement of the code at the end of the page isn't absolutely required, it is a web design best practice.

To place the code into the template:

1. Locate the **footer.php** file.
2. Towards the end of the week in the code, there should be a pair of lines:
   </body>
   </html>
3. Create a new blank line above these two lines of code
4. Paste the script provided by Google onto the new blank line.

NOTE: If you change to a different template, you must remember to re-insert the code into the new template.

Adding Google Analytics to Your Non-Blog Website

Adding the GA code to any webpage is the same as Steps 2 & 3 of the process for Wordpress templates, except you must make sure that the code is included on every page that you want to track, and you will have to add them one at a time.

Tracking Multiple Domains

Your GA account allows you to track multiple domains from one Google account. To add a domain to your Google analytics account, select "Create New Account" in the "My Analytics Accounts" drop-down menu. From there, follow all the steps from creating your first account. Note that the code that you will be inserting onto each of the pages will be slightly different.

Understanding Google Analytics Reports

After installing the GA tracking code into your blog (or website), you can log into your account's dashboard to monitor visitor activity.

Here is a breakdown of the data provided in your Google Analytics dashboard:

Site Usage

This is where you can see the top-level stats of your website at a glance: total visits in the time period selected; total number of individual page views; pages per visit; bounce rate; average time visitors spend on your site, and the percentage of total visitors that are first-time visitors to your site.

Visitors Overview

This is a repeat of the top-level chart for daily counts of visitors.

Map Overlay

This area shows you geographically where your visitors are coming from. This can be especially useful for locating and targeting your fans.

Traffic Sources Overview

This chart shows from which sites visitors are reaching your site. If you notice a high percentage of visitors are coming from a particular area, you can focus your marketing efforts there.

Content Overview

The overview chart shows which pages within your site are getting the most attention. This information can be useful in deciding where to place important information or which portions of your content are most interesting to your fans.

NOTES

NOTES

WEEK 4: SOCIAL MEDIA PRIMER

Social Media = Engagement

The evolution of the internet as a marketing tool has made more opportunities available to musicians than ever before. Websites like Facebook, Twitter, Google+, and dozens of others help people connect and communicate in new ways, making it possible to reach thousands of people in a very short amount of time.

If used smartly, social media can be highly beneficial to musicians eager to build their fan bases and increase their music sales. In fact, willingness to master the basics of social media and internet marketing will separate successful musicians from those destined to struggle.

PART 1: Web 2.0 Defined

You probably have heard people using the term Web 2.0 and you may not have known what they were talking about. It's an important principle to grasp before we dive into Social Media sites as they all operate in a Web 2.0 environment.

Main Features of Web 2.0

The following are Web 2.0's 3 main features:

1. Social Networking Websites (Twitter, Google+, Facebook and YouTube);
2. Wikis (such as Wikipedia) where groups of people contribute;
3. Tagging/Social Bookmarking (creating tags on blog posts, photos and geographical locations).

As a musician with a presence within the Web 2.0 landscape, you can connect on a more personal level with new media and fans. By creating strong social networking profiles and keeping them fed with great content and two-way engagement, you will create many more opportunities through which potential fans can learn about you and your music.

The Future Conversation

The web evolves at a breakneck pace, and there is a constant shift in the conversation. I'm giving you a lot to digest in this chapter. But I would be irresponsible if I didn't point out the upcoming trends and conversations I hear at major music conferences worldwide.

1. **Mobile**—Optimize your site for handheld devices.
2. **"The Cloud"**
3. **Klout.com**—Raise your "status" as an influencer

Mobile

As phones keep evolving, and as connecting to the Internet and using social media from our mobile devices becomes easier and easier, you need to keep in mind how you look on your mobile phone. More people are using smartphones and iPads as part of their everyday interactions. Your website should be optimized for mobile browsing. Ask your web developer to make sure he has handled this task, or test it yourself from a few different types of devices. Also be aware that text messaging is a very powerful way to capture and engage fans.

Movie Time

Watch Carla Lynne Hall, the co-author of my book *Musician's Roadmap to Facebook and Twitter* and I talk to Cyber PR® artist Jennings about how she uses text messaging to get fans to her live performances.
http://bit.ly/JenningsMobile

TIP: Flash players are not readable on Apple devices (iPhones, iPads or iPod Touches), so avoid having a Flash player for your music. I highly recommend using *Soundcloud.com* as your player. It works on all handheld devices.

"The Cloud"

Tech-minded music industry leaders have been talking about "the cloud" for a few years. And Spotify, which launched in July, 20011 in the U.S., is now the most pervasive example in the music space.

When you hear the term "the cloud," it refers to data that is being stored on your behalf, but not on your computer. Cloud computing is a service rather than a tangible product, and it is the process by which shared resources, software and information are provided to computers and other devices over a network (the Internet). Simply put, back in the day, if a car ran over your laptop, or if you got a bad virus, you would be in a world of pain. Now with the cloud, your photos, music and documents are safe, as they are not stored locally.

Some examples of cloud computing are...

Google Docs—These can be accessed by anyone, anywhere.

Yahoo! Mail—You can check your Yahoo! e-mail from any computer.

Spotify—Your music collection (and any additional music you want to listen to) is accessible anywhere.

Klout.com

Just being on social media is not enough. That's what this chapter is all about. You need to join the conversations, interact, and push content out consistently. This will make you an influencer. And, being an influencer is what will move the needle for you.

Klout.com is a website that "scores" your effectiveness online. All you need to do is sign up and add your Twitter, Facebook, YouTube, and Foursquare (and more) accounts to it, and Klout will serve up a number based on your interactions and relevancy to your online community. If your Klout score is healthy, your fan engagement and calls to action should be well responded to. If your Klout score is low, you should follow the guidelines suggested by the site to increase your score. Klout is not the only social media ecosystem gage out there. But following the site's suggestions makes the process of raising your profile online easy.

Watering Your Social Media Garden

One thing to keep in mind is that Social Media is much like a garden. It takes consistent cultivation and weeding to make it thrive. Just planting once and leaving it alone will not make your garden grow. Joining multiple social media sites will help you spread your word and connect with others. Once you participate in a two-way conversation, you will get support from other users on these sites.

Each social media site has its own protocol that you must follow. As you get to know the rules, you will start to reap the benefits of tying into each community.

The #1 complaint that I get from artists is they do not want to get involved with multiple websites. They say it's just too much, they don't have time, and they don't like it! If you are among this group resistant to using a variety of social media sites, I understand your feelings and I sympathize. However, you will ultimately be left behind in the dust to die in obscurity if you cannot change with the times. In order to be on the court as an artist you must participate in the game and you must be on at least a few sites.

I will outline the sites that I think are critical to get you started, in the order that I suggest diving in.

The Context: Your 3 Communities

Many musicians really resist using social media, and that's understandable. As an artist, time spent managing social media takes away from the creative time you'd rather spend playing. But put that aside if you can, and let's approach it from a different perspective. Let's think about your fan base.

Your fan base is not just one lumped-together group of people. It is, in fact, 3 very separate communities. And the fact is, you need to think about how you approach each one of these communities differently.

Community #1: *Your Super Fans*

These are fans who are primarily your **Live Audience**. You know them by name. If you play out, they attend your shows regularly and buy many things you have to offer (not just your music). If you have a street team, your Live Audience is on it, and they evangelize strongly on your behalf.

Community #2: *Engaged Fans*

These fans are your **Active Online Audience**. They are newsletter subscribers, blog readers, video watchers, RSS subscribers, and active social media friends who frequently comment and engage with you on Facebook, Twitter, YouTube, and more.

Community #3: *Ambient Fans*

These fans are your **Passive Online Audience**. They are your social media friends who are aware of you via Twitter, Facebook, etc. but don't actively communicate with you and may not have ever even heard your music (yet).

There are many different sub-categories within these communities to tack onto this list, but these are the primary three.

The problem is, most musicians only have one strategy for marketing and promoting to 3 totally separate groups. The way you maintain your relationship with each of these communities requires a different strategy, because you have varying degrees of engagement with each of them.

The way you create and develop your relationships can be easily organized using social media. Members of Community #3 may read a tweet here and there, whereas those from Community #1 will read every blog post you write. This is why you need to have an integrated social media presence.

GETTING STARTED—
UNDERSTANDING SOCIAL MEDIA
IN LESS THAN 15 MINUTES

Before you attempt to dive into this new and complex world, I highly recommend that you spend a few minutes at this website: *http://www.commoncraft.com*

This site has produced a few short movies that will explain the basic terms of Web 2.0 and social media in plain English.

These videos are short and brilliant. I suggest you start with these. I will reference others throughout this book.

1. Social Networking in Plain English:
   http://www.commoncraft.com/video-social-networking

2. Social Media in Plain English:
   http://www.commoncraft.com/socialmedia

3. Social Bookmarking in Plain English:
   http://www.commoncraft.com/bookmarking-plain-english

4. Wikis in Plain English:
   http://www.commoncraft.com/video-wikis-plain-english

PART 2: Social Media Must-Haves: Facebook/Facebook Fan Pages; Twitter; Flickr & Podcasts

A strong social media presence doesn't happen over-night. Each social media environment has its own protocol you need to follow as well as its own feel, mood, and emphasis. As you get to know each one and build a following, you'll start to reap the benefits of communicating within each community.

I suggest you dig in and get very comfortable with one social media platform before you join a second, then a third, etc. Eventually, you need to join multiple networks so you can get more exposure and more opportunities to attract fans and sell music. But if you build up your social media presence one site at a time, you will prevent yourself from getting overwhelmed.

Facebook

Now that you understand the social media basics, we will start with the mother of all social media sites: Facebook.

Over 800,000,000 people worldwide are currently on Facebook. And recently, Facebook has been getting much friendlier for music promotion. There are now some great tools available to make your Facebook efforts shine and bring your music to the forefront.

Chances are, you probably already have a personal profile on Facebook (and hopefully a fan page too!). But if not, this Week you can fix that.

Every single time I talk to a group of musicians, a hand goes up, and I get the following question:

Do I really need to have a Facebook personal profile as well as a Fan Page?

The answer is, "Yes." And here's why:

1. There are probably people in your life who care about the events in your personal life. These people want to share what's happening with you and with your family and tag photos of you in personal groups. These friends may be fans of your music, but may not care so much about your constant fan page updates, MP3 giveaways and touring announcements.

2. You may want to maintain a personal profile to keep in touch with real friends and family. This is important when you want to share information that might not be appropriate to share with your fan base.

3. Personal pages max out at 5,000. The maximum amount of friends you can have on your personal profile is 5,000. This means if you friend more than 5,000 people, bands, and brands on your personal profile, you will have to un-friend some people in order to add new friends or start another personal profile, which Facebook does not consider "legal" behavior. Having a fan page is crucial, because it actually allows you to have more than 5,000 friends.

Here's the problem: You may have started promoting yourself on Facebook before Facebook Fan Pages were available, so your Facebook fans and your "real"* friends are muddled together.

I'm not implying that your fans are not your "real" friends; I'm just saying there is probably a separation that you make, and that the information you share with each group could be different.

Widgets

Another common social media tool you will see are widgets. I'm going to be referring to "widgets" throughout this book. A widget (sometimes called a badge) is simply a small piece of code that you can copy and paste into the HTML (programming) of any site. And when you update a widget in one place, it updates all over the web. You can put the same widget on Facebook, your blog, and on your own site. Then you can update it once and it will be updated all over the internet. My favorite widgets are available here: *bit.ly/reverbfreebribe* and *bit.ly/pledgefreebribe*

FACEBOOK FOR NEWBIES: HOW TO SET UP A FACEBOOK FAN PAGE

Here is a quick rundown for newbies of how to create a fan page as a band/musician.

Step 1: Create a Band/Artist profile.

Go to *http://www.facebook.com/pages/create/php*.

Step 2: Click on the "Artist, Band or Public Figure" box.

Step 3: Select "Musician/Band" from the drop-down category list.

Step 4: Enter your name.

After you enter your name, check the box next to "I agree to Facebook Pages Terms," then click "Get Started."

You are now off to the races! The rest is pretty self explanatory. Upload your photo for your main user icon, your bio, band members, additional photos, and details.

Locating Your Fan Page

After you create your fan page, finding its location might seem fairly obvious, but the process can be difficult for many musicians. Here's how you can find it:

1. Type your page name into the search bar at the top of any Facebook page.
2. Select it from the drop-down menu that appears.
3. Visit the page.

Ariel's Top 5 Facebook Apps

What are Apps?

Apps (short for applications) are tools created by third-party developers that cooperate with websites such as Twitter and Facebook. On Facebook, apps are cool tools you can add to your page so you can display features such as music, photos, and videos.

For example, **My Band** is an app developed by ReverbNation that allows you to put your music on the Facebook platform.

As you likely know, the iPhone and the iPad have become wildly popular because of apps. Some are free and some cost money, and they are fun because they make your social media and your smartphone experience customizable.

Thousands of app developers create apps for countless uses. There are so many, your head can spin. Facebook has a great page that explains how to help you with apps. FAQs are here:

http://www.facebook.com/help/?page=25

Here are the Facebook apps I recommend as essentials for musicians along with links to where you can download them:

1. RootMusic BandPage

I am a huge fan of RootMusic's BandPage app. They have 2 versions of their BandPages: a free options and a paid option ($1.99/mo). You don't have to know any code or html to put together a branded, professional-looking page. Their BandPages allows artists to upload music, photos, and videos for fan enjoyment. What really sets this app apart is the ability to put a large banner across the top and customize the color scheme of the app to fit your image and branding. This brilliant integration allows for increased interaction between musicians and fans.

http://bit.ly/RootMusicBandPage

2. ReverbNation Band Profile

Musicians, artists, and bands can post unlimited songs for streaming or download, add bios and band photos, sell music, and have friends share music to start conversations with their friends. (Now that's viral marketing for you!) This app also includes links to your homepage,

and you can add up to 30 of your songs (full length) to your Facebook Fan Page. And the best part: it provides great stats to track song-play activity.
http://on.fb.me/ReverbNationBandProfile

3. FanBridge Fan Page

FanBridge—known for their newsletter management services—bought DamnTheRadio since the last edition of this book and have made some significant improvements to the Fan Page app. Like the RootMusic and ReverbNation apps, FanBridge's Fan Page app allows the artist to upload content like music, videos, and pictures. FanBridge has also partnered with Ecosystem so you can promote and sell merchandise, tickets, crowdfunding projects and more, all within the app.
http://bit.ly/FanBridgeFanPage

4. Bandcamp

Bandcamp's app is a great resource for any Bandcamp user. (If you don't use Bandcamp, I highly recommend it.) This app will pull all the media and information from your already-set-up Bandcamp page and automatically load it in to the app for you. With this app, fans can listen to all of the music you have uploaded and purchase this music directly from the app.
http://bit.ly/BandcampApp

5. CD Baby Store

This app is a must for anyone who uses CD Baby for their distribution. With this app, everything you have for sale on CD Baby can now be purchased directly from

an app on your Facebook fan page. Your fans will be able to browse through all of the albums you have for sale, preview the tracks, share them with friends and then buy them all in one spot).
http://on.fb.me/CDBabyStore

Google+

Google+ is a new social media feature created by Google that can be linked up to any Gmail account and used to communicate with friends and other contacts. It allows you to put your contacts into different groups and choose to which you send out specific information, such as status message updates, etc. At the time this book was published, Google+ did not yet have sophisticated capabilities in terms of professional marketing techniques. But I wanted to mention it because it could potentially be a social media tool you might want to add to your arsenal in the future.

Twitter

Twitter is an ingenious solution that will give your fans more of you, connect you to conversations with people, and it takes less than 3 minutes a day to use effectively—without your computer—and it can be synched to Facebook and your website to triple its effectiveness!

Need a Visual? Watch These Videos:

Twitter in Plain English:
http://www.commoncraft.com/twitter

Twitter Search in Plain English:
http://www.commoncraft.com/twitter-search

5 Reasons Why You Should Care about Twitter

1. It's free, easy to join, and so easy to use. All you do is "tweet" (write) small texts of 140 characters or less from your phone or from your computer.

2. It is the third fastest-growing social media site on-line and now has over 200 million users. Facebook is first with over 800 million (as of December, 2011).

3. Your fan base will feel more connected to you, and they can interact directly with you via tweets, replies, and direct messages. But you don't *have* to follow or interact with everyone who follows you!

4. It will help you build your brand. It's an amazing way to quickly connect with lots of people you'd never meet otherwise. As musicians, you want to spread the word to as many people as possible, and Twitter allows you connect to thousands of people at once.

5. Twitter feeds/widgets are easy to install, and you can drop them onto your own website or your blog. This way your fans can keep up with you from whichever site they choose to spend their time on and your content stays fresh across social media sites.

Twitter Terms:

Twitter has its own vocabulary, and the key to understanding the platform is learning the Twitter language. Here are some terms to get you started:

Tweet—An individual Twitter message must be 140 characters or less.

It can:

1. Report what you are doing/Answer the question "What's happening?"

2. Allow you to share links to content (music, photos, blog posts, articles, videos etc).

3. Help you engage with others by using @'s (more on this to follow).

Following—The people whose Twitter messages you follow.

Followers—The people who are following your Twitter messages.

Twitter Handle—This refers to your Twitter username it begins with an "AT" @CyberPR/@MusicSuccessin9.

Twitstream / Tweetstream / Twitter Stream—
The collective stream of Twitter messages (tweets) sent by you and the people that you're following. No one's twitstream is exactly alike.

RT (or "ReTweet")—Quoting or repeating someone else's tweet (Twitter message) in your tweet stream.

@Replies—Also called "at replies," these are the tweets in which your Twitter name is mentioned by others. Whenever someone tweets (or ReTweets) your Twitter name within their Twitter message, you can keep track of these mentions with a single click.

Direct Messages (also "DMs")—Private tweets between you and another person. You can only send DMs to people who are following you.

Favorites—Tweets that you have marked as favorite, marked by a little gold star.

Search—Twitter search engine on your Twitter page which can be used to find words and phrases used in tweets. For more advanced searches, use: http://search.Twitter.com.

Trending Topics—The most tweeted-about words or phrases at the present time. This list is located on the right sidebar of your home Twitter page. Trending topics often correspond with current events. When marked with a hash tag, "#" (also called a pound sign), the keyword can be easily tracked at a later time.

Lists—A group of users that you can curate by trend, location, theme, etc.

Listed—Shows who has included you. You can follow entire lists.

Hash Tags—A hash tag (#) is used on Twitter when people want to post information about a particular topic or an event going on—so it makes it easy for others to find. You will see them pop up when large events are happening (or on popular TV and sporting nights).

Example: #SXSW11, #ElectionNight, #MadMen, #Superbowl

When a hash tag is included before a particular phrase, others interested in tweets related to that phrase can easily search and find them.

TIP: Adding a hash tag to your tweet is easy; just type "#" and create any one you want!

TWITTER IN 9 STEPS

STEP 1: Think About Your User Name (Handle) First.

When you go to set up an account, don't just pick a name you like. **Use the name that matches your website, your Facebook profile, and your Myspace page for consistency.** And remember, whichever name you choose on Twitter becomes Google-icious too.

Definition: Google-icious **(a word I made up!)**

Your ability to be found on search engines. Social media is the best way to become Google-icious. When you consistently use the tools provided by social media, you are automatically more findable on Google and other search engines.

STEP 2: Sign Up.

Twitter will take you through a few sign-up steps where you'll enter your username, password and e-mail. Twitter will search your e-mail address book to see if the people you know are already using it. You will also have the option of sending e-mail invites to your friends.

TIP: Take some time and set up your profile properly. You probably had a Website made for your music, and that involved spending money. You put a lot of thought into it. Here's a chance to have a free Website. Put up a good profile picture. (That's the little, tiny square picture that goes next to all your messages.) Add your pitch and link to your Web page in your profile under the "Profile" section.

STEP 3: Link Your Mobile Phone.

Enter your mobile phone number...if you want to accept tweets via texts. Do this only if you have a good text-messaging plan and a high tolerance for receiving loads of texts on your mobile phone. You'll have the option of receiving tweets to your phone from only a few select people, so don't worry about your phone blowing up if you follow lots of people from your account. You can also edit this list down.

Many people have smartphones (iPhones, Droids, and Black-berrys) and there are great apps you can install to manage your Twitter accounts too. Tweetie, ÜberTwitter, Tweetdeck and the iPhone app created by Twitter are all great.

TIP: If you have a smartphone, install a Twitter app and tweet on the go.

STEP 4: Search Keywords.

Go to the search field on the Dashboard and start searching key words that are important to you, topics you are interested in, words about the music you play, whether those words be genre- or instrument- related. When you find interesting tweets in those searches, follow the people who are saying those things that interest you. This gives you a great jump-ing-off point and an easy way to find new people to follow.

STEP 5: Link Twitter to Update Your Facebook Status.

Go to *http://bit.ly/TwitterTweetFB* so you can link your Twitter page directly to your Facebook profile. This way, you'll be able to update your status on Facebook by using Twitter from your phone or computer.

STEP 6: Follow Lots of People.

Twitter does not work in a vacuum, so the key is to follow at least 50 people. Start by following me at *http://twitter.com/cyberpr* and *http://twitter.com/musicsuccessin9*.
You can also follow my cat at *http://twitter.com/thehuntercat*.

STEP 7: Tweet 3 Times per Day.

Just keep answering the question, "What's happening?" And share links your community may like. At first, you may feel really awkward telling people what you are doing, but do it anyway. You'll get into the swing of it once people start responding to you and engaging.

TIP: Don't over-hype yourself. If all your tweets are statements like "Buy my album!" or "Come to my show!" you're not going to build a audience that trusts you.

STEP 8: @People You Like, RT Tweets You Like and DM.

To comment on tweets you like or have a reaction to, or to connect directly with someone, just tweet @ and then their username. So if you want to say something directly to Derek Sivers, type @Sivers and then your message. This will turn up in the Replies section of Derek's Twitter dashboard, and he will see your comment. But so will everyone else! This is a public message that everyone on Twitter will see.

If you like something you read and you want to share it with your followers, ReTweet it by typing "RT" before the tweet then simply copy and paste it, add your own comment or just use the RT button on your dashboard, and send.

Example: "RT **@CyberPR** I just updated my Musicians Guide To Understanding PR for today's Music Business list on Amazon Enjoy! *http://bit.ly/cyberpramzn*"

To send someone a direct, private message, go to your dashboard on Twitter and click where it says "Direct Messages" over in the right-side column. Then choose the person to whom you want to send a message from the pull-down menu at the top of the page. **A direct message is a private message.** Only the user you choose will see it.

TIP: You can only DM people who you are following & who are following you back, otherwise you will have to publicly **@mention** them.

STEP 9: Use a Twitter Management Tool

Harnessing the power of Twitter can be really empowering when you know how to do it right. These 3 tools / apps are so easy, it's almost impossible to mess them up.

»   HootSuite
    http://hootsuite.com

»   SocialOomph
    http://www.socialoomph.com

»   TweetDeck
    http://www.tweetdeck.com

EXERCISE: MAKE YOUR TWITTER MATCH YOUR BRAND

Start a Twitter account for your band or for yourself.

If you are registering with a band name, I also suggest registering your first and last name so you will have 2 accounts. One can redirect to the other (to see what I mean go to *http://www.twitter.com/arielhyatt*) and see what I did.

If you already have a Twitter account make sure you follow these steps:

STEP 1: Add your pitch as your description, with a link back to your website and an offer to sign up to your newsletter list.

STEP 2: Make sure your background profile colors match your website, Facebook, and Google+ colors, and that your photo matches your main image on your website. (A logo can stand out even more than a photo.)

STEP 3: Make sure you are following at least 50 people (including me, please: *http://www.twitter.com/cyberpr*).

STEP 4: Post to our closed Mastermind site so we can all follow and support each other.

STEP 5: Please post other suggestions for who to follow as well!

STEP 6: Schedule with HootSuite and SocialOomph. Both offer online tools for scheduling Twitter messages and Facebook status messages. By scheduling some of your tweets and status messages, you can free up your time for other things...like practicing music!

For iPhones and Android phones: I suggest HootSuite and Tweetdeck, available at the app store for download.

Flickr: Your Visual Photoblog

Are you too lazy to blog? Does blogging feel like a huge, annoying, daunting task that is evocative of being a kid again and getting a giant homework assignment?

Well, fear not. I've got a great, easy blogging solution:

http://www.flickr.com

First—Watch the Video, "Photo Sharing in Plain English:" *http://www.commoncraft.com/photosharing*

They say a picture is worth a thousand words, and it's true.

Flickr is an easy photo-sharing site. And Yahoo owns it, so millions of potential new fans are waiting for you to discover them and make friends. Flickr works in many ways just like Facebook. You create a profile, upload your main image, join groups, and make friends. You can also direct-message people and leave comments on any photo you like.

Photos tell a complete story of you!

On Flickr you can post photos of things other than your band activities—vacations, kids, your hometown, and hobbies—to show your fans you are a well-rounded individual. If you go to conferences, this is a great way to connect with people you meet. (Remember, the most interesting thing for people to see and talk about is themselves.)

CREATE A VIP PHOTO-SHARING EXPERIENCE FOR YOUR FANS

Your photos can be marked "private" so only approved fans and friends can see certain photos. Flickr lets you choose which sets to share. I suggest creating a VIP area of fun/special photos that only gives access to your registered fans/friends/street team as an added bonus for them to link to you.

Top 10 Reasons Why Musicians Should Use Flickr

1. *It helps you build your fan base.* (This is the #1 reason you need to use it!) One of the best things about Flickr is that you can search to join groups and make new friends, fans, and contacts.

2. *It's easy.* If all the writing that blogging entails overwhelms you, Flickr is a perfect choice. All you need to do is upload photos from your cell phone or digital camera, create brief captions, tag things properly, and...voilà!

3. *You will make a personal connection with your fans.* It's a great way for them to see other dimensions of you and get "behind the scenes."

4. *You can create multiple photo sets.* Break sets of photos up by categories within your site, so people who are interested in live music could go to your live shots, people who are interested in candid shots of the band having fun can go to those shots, etc.

5. *You can start your own Flickr group and get known.* In addition to your personal page, you can start a group and invite others to join. You can

75

create groups for "backstage shots," "on-the-road photos," or "musicians and their dogs." Get creative and start a new community that no one has thought of yet. You can also join Flickr groups and network with others by leaving comments on their photos.

6. *You can create sets that will drive traffic by linking to other groups.* Examples include Music festivals, Live Shots, Fan Shots etc. I've included a list to get you started later in this Week.

7. *Flickr is great for promoting your own site.* As people come and browse your photos, include links to your site to drive traffic to you.

8. *You will be able to get the cutest/coolest business cards on Earth.* Flickr works with a site called Moo, and they make the greatest cards with assorted photos on each—a cool and creative way to share your info: *http://www.moo.com/flickr*

BONUS REASON: *You Can Cross Post Photo Sets on Facebook.* For every photo set you create, cross post on Facebook photos.

Some Photo Set Ideas

Here are some ideas for grouping your newly uploaded photos:

Fans in the Audience—You can create a whole album of just fans by taking pictures of fans at your shows. Your fans are interested in themselves (and each other) as well as in you and your music!

Posed Shots Of Fans—Ask your most loyal followers to send in great photos of themselves with captions they create. This will keep your fans coming back to see themselves.

Food—Take photos of all the food you eat on the road or take a picture of your lunch every day and make a photo plates diary.

Behind the Scenes—Take pictures of you in the studio, loading your gear into a club, writing music, buying instruments, etc., and add comments about what the life of a musician is from behind the scenes.

Band Candids—Outtakes from photo shoots and videos. Live shots.

Music Festivals / Conferences—When you go to CMJ, SXSW etc. you can maximize your experience by covering all events. Many of these music festivals have their own Flickr sites so you can upload those photo sets directly to each Flickr group and use them to network with the people that were there.

TIP: How to add a contact: Simply click on the image of the person (the Buddy Icon) you want to add and a menu will pop up and direct you! Loads of questions can be answered here if you get stuck: *http://www.flickr.com/help/faq*

SOME FLICKR GROUPS TO CHECK OUT AND JOIN:

Ariel Publicity & Cyber PR®—Be Our Friend!
http://www.flickr.com/photos/ArielPublicityPR

Band Publicity Photos:
http://tinyurl.com/FlickrBandShot

Music Directory:
http://www.flickr.com/groups/MusicDirectory

Girls With Guitars:
http://www.flickr.com/groups/GirlsWithGuitars

Music Makers:
http://www.flickr.com/groups/MusicMakers

My Love Affair With Music:
http://www.flickr.com/groups/MusicLovers/

Live Music Photography:
http://tinyurl.com/FlickrLiveMusic

Live Music:
http://www.flickr.com/groups/Live-Music/

Instagram

If you really love to share photos, a great new app is available for iPhone called Instagram. It makes it easy to share and edit photos on social media. You can find it at *http://instagr.am/* or in the iTunes App Store.

I'd love to join your groups and see your photos, so please do include me as a friend once you get started. I can be found at *http://www.flickr.com/ArielPublicityPR*

Podcasts

Movie Time

Let's start with another great movie!
http://commoncraft.com/podcasting

The fastest way to get involved with Podcasting is to join **Music Alley** from Mevio (which used to be known as the Podsafe Music Network).

When you become a podsafe artist you are allowing podcasters to use your tracks in their shows without worrying about clearance issues. This means you are giving away your tracks for them to use royalty-free, in exchange for podcast play and promotion.

I am a huge fan and advocate of podcasting, and the podcasting community is both tight knit and wonderful.

Hundreds of podcasters use **Music Alley** to get music for their podcasts, and the bonus is you can see who is logging in, choosing your music, and adding it to their podcasts.

To join Music Alley:

STEP 1: **Sign Up.**

Go to *http://music.mevio.com* and click on the green box that says, "Artists submit your music and watch your fans and CD sales grow."

STEP 2: **Complete the Artist Registration Form**

You will create a username and a password for yourself here and use this in the future to check which podcasters are including you on their shows.

STEP 3: **Monitor Your Podcast Plays.**

When you get played, there will be a link to the podcast so you can check it out!

I highly suggest that you log on and listen to the podcast so you can hear yourself and hear what the podcaster had to say about you. The only way to forge authentic relationships with podcasters is by listening to their shows.

HOW TO THANK A PODCASTER WHO PLAYS YOUR MUSIC

Podcasters are hobbyists who work very hard to create fun, high-quality podcasts because they love music. The best thing you can do to ingratiate yourself with this community is to thank them for including you. They will love you for this and play more of your music in the future.

1. *Record a Custom Station ID as a Thank You:*

   » Create an MP3 with the podcast name.

   » The script can be creative but should include the following key points:

   » "Hey, this is (Band / Artist Name) and you're listening to our new record (Album Title) on (name of podcast). Check us out at (Band Website / Facebook fan page)."

   » The more creative the better; play music, make funny voices, etc., but try to keep it under 20 seconds.

2. *Acknowledge the Creator of The Podcast By Doing One of the Following:*

   » Tweet about the podcast with a link to it.

   » Blog about the podcast on your website's blog or on Tumblr.

   » Post the link and a thank-you to your status updates on Facebook.

   » Leave a message on the podcaster's VM thanking them for the add. (Many podcasters have telephone #s listed on their sites with answering machines hooked up to them so you can leave a message. Most of the time they will play the message on another podcast and also add another song to their playlist, so this is very beneficial!)

» Add a link back to their site on your website or on your blogroll.

» Review the podcast on iTunes—this is the best way to thank a podcaster as well-reviewed podcasts move up the charts at iTunes.

TIP: Remember to let the podcaster know you reviewed his/her podcast on iTunes via e-mail, Facebook or Twitter. Spread the love!

NOTES

WEEK 5: THE MUSICIAN'S GUIDE TO YOUTUBE

YouTube is a critical social media site to include in your arsenal of social media/online marketing techniques. There is no way to refute the power of video. YouTube is the second largest online search engine. It has hundreds of millions of users from around the world and is localized in 25 countries across 43 languages.

In 2006, Google bought YouTube for $1.65 billion. So, now YouTube operates as a subsidiary of Google (which is of course the largest online search engine). It's important to understand how they relate to each other in order to maximize your presence.

Here are some mind-blowing YouTube stats:

» 48 hours of video are uploaded every minute, resulting in nearly 8 years of content uploaded every day, which results in over 3 billion views daily.

» More than 50% of videos on YouTube have been rated or include comments from the YouTube community.

YouTube is a Social Network.

YouTube is an interactive Social Network just like Facebook or Twitter, and you are encouraged to make friends with other users. I'm often shocked that artists expect to simply post a video on YouTube, make no friends on the site, watch no one else's videos and still "go viral." Making friends, leaving comments, and thumbing up as many videos as you can are key moves on the YouTube platform.

If you start looking around online, you will see people leading you back to their YouTube channels all over the Internet. If you see links to YouTube on people's Facebook, Twitter, websites or blogs, head on over, subscribe to their channels, watch videos, leave comments, and make friends. That's social!

TIP: Being active on Youtube is a great newsletter-building strategy. Once you engage someone on YouTube and get into a conversation with him, you can ask if you can add him to your newsletter.

5 Compelling Reasons to Use YouTube

1. Market yourself and your music on the world's second-largest search engine.

2. Interact with fans, music professionals and other artists.

3. Create videos that appear in Google search results. Be Google-icious!

4. Attract more fans.

5. Become a Viral Sensation!

Before You Dive in ...

Watch What is Already Working, and Follow!

Before you upload a well-produced video of yourself performing or pay for a multi-camera shoot, I strongly caution you to take a look at what is "going viral" on YouTube. They make this easy by posting the most viewed video here: *http://www.youtube.com/charts.* I suggest you watch the most viewed videos in the music categories for several weeks and see if you can decipher a trend or come up with an idea that might fit for you on this most-viewed chart list before you outline your own content strategy or add to it.

Think about Your Audience.

Keep in mind that many people watch videos while they are at work. And people pass along videos that are funny, amusing or interesting to them in some form or fashion.

Make Your Video Less than 3 Minutes

Why? We live in an A.D.D. world and anything longer will reduce your chance of the entire video being watched.

Always Include a Call to Action (CTA)

Remember, in order to get people to take action, you need to tell them what to do. Add a Call to Action (CTA) to every video you post. A CTA could be "Follow us on Twitter," "Like us on Facebook" or "Visit Our Site." Only include ONE CTA in each video you post so you don't confuse your audience. Without a CTA, you are leaving potential traffic on the table. The whole point of videos is to drive traffic back to your site. (You remember that, yes?)

It Doesn't Have to Be Fancy or Expensive to Be Viral!

Look at the charts. There are a lot of videos on YouTube that are lo-fi and not "produced." And they get millions of views.

Remember the Purpose of Videos.

The reason you make videos in the first place is important to remember! It is not just to get a lot of views (that's just the beginning); it is to get people to **take an action**. Whether that action is coming back to your website or following you on Facebook or Twitter, it's critical to remember why you made your video. Keep your eye on the end goal and make sure you constantly measure your videos' effectiveness.

Know What People are Searching for.

Remember that YouTube is a search engine. This means people are searching for things that they already know and love on YouTube. So, including content that people already know is crucial, because they are already looking for it! Here is a site (set up by YouTube) where you can actually research exactly what people are searching for word for word:

https://ads.youtube.com/keyword_tool

Cover Songs Really Work!

A few months ago, I interviewed YouTube cover song phenomenon Tiffany Alvord. She explained her formula for how she gets millions of viewers to watch her videos:

http://bit.ly/ViralVidTiffany

There was quite a reaction to this interview. I was met with a lot of sneering, older musicians saying, "I'm not a hot, young teen. I can't do that." If you are having this same reaction, my answer to you is, "Yes you can!"

Granted, there is a trend on YouTube of many young teens creating videos of cover songs from their bedrooms. And some of these videos garner millions of views. However, talented grownups can do this too!

Here is an example of a Cyber PR® artist, Jane Lui, who uses covers beautifully to attract fans (and she is well above 16!):

http://www.youtube.com/LuieLand

Before you start writing off this strategy as something for tweens, think again. Fans that already know and love many songs that are near and dear to their hearts may actually find out about you if you create a cover song that captivates them!

HOW TO SET UP YOUR YOUTUBE CHANNEL IN 5 STEPS

It's easy to set up your very own channel at YouTube. Just go to YouTube.com and press the big button on the top of the page that says "Create Account."

You can then choose a username for your channel.

If you have a Gmail account (because, again, Google owns YouTube), it will assign your Gmail username as your channel name, and then you can edit it.

1. Be Consistent Across Platforms

Make sure your channel name matches your website and your username on Facebook and Twitter. Ideally, you should make your user name your band's/artist's name. If that name is unavailable, add something like "music" or "official" onto your user name.

2. Your Channel Name Should Include Keywords

Remember, YouTube is owned by Google, and keywords are very important. So, if you are not using your artist name, think about which keywords fit you and your music.

3. Choose Musician Channel

Login and go to your page. Click on the "Settings" tab at the top of the page and select "Musician" as the channel type.

4. **Choose Your Themes & Colors**

Next to "Settings" you will see the "Channel Design" tab. Here you can choose different colors, upload a background image, and select your text and hyperlink colors.

TIP: Make sure your colors match your overall branding: your website; blog; Facebook account; Twitter account.

TIP: It's very hard to read darkly-colored fonts against a black background. Choose colors that are easy on the eyes for the sake of your visitors. And remember, white is never a bad choice. (Google and YouTube are white for a reason. This color is effective.)

5. **Upload Your Videos**

Go to the "My Videos and Playlists" tab and click on the blue button on the top left that says "New." Select "video upload" and start adding your videos.

Optimizing Your Channel

Titles are Key.

I've been reading a lot of YouTube studies, and it turns out that the single biggest contributing factor to your success on a video click through will be directly related to how you title your video.

TIP: Make sure that the title of each of your videos includes your artist or band name, song title, and any other relevant information.

TIP: If it's not a straight-ahead music video, create a title that will make the viewer want to watch the video. Something captivating and catchy is key. (However, remember that it must relate back to the actual video.)

The Description Box is Crucial.

The description box is critical to optimization of your channel. Always start with your URL at the very beginning of the description box and don't forget to include *http://* or else it will not show up as a hyperlink. And it's not a bad idea to add this link (or a link to your Facebook, Twitter, etc. at the end of the description as well).

Select a Proper Video Category.

This will more than likely be "Music." But it could be "humor" or "education" too. Remember to think about which best fits your content!

Tag Thoroughly.

Google ranks tags, so always start with the tag that is the most important. If you are adding a title that is more than one word, put it in quotes—i.e., "Sympathy For The Devil"—or else the words will become individual tags. Don't overdo the number of tags. (Google frowns upon over-tagging, so keep it to 7 or 8 at the most). Some tag ideas: artist/band name; song name; any related artists names (especially if you add a cover); similar artists (so that when people type in an artist they like they will come across your video); genres of music; hometown; names of all band members; producer; themes in video, etc.

TIP: Don't overdo it! Your build out will take some time. YouTube moderates user activity closely, much as Facebook moderates its own user activity. If you receive a notice to stop sending messages, adding friends, etc., STOP, or else your account will be deleted. And you don't want that!

Subscribe to Other Channels.

Subscribing to other channels can help you go a long way. Search for keywords that match yours. Start by subscribing to channels of similar artists or artists that influenced you or that you sound like. After you have subscribed to your favorite artist's channels, start subscribing to their fans' channels by going to the artist's channel and locating the "Subscribers" box. This will be a good place to start adding friends.

Add Videos as Favorites.

Love the video? Just click on that little heart. Keep in mind that these videos will be added to your "Favorites" section on your channel.

Comment on Videos.

Respond to other people's comments, just as you would respond to others' comments on Facebook.

Rate the Comments.

You can click on the "thumbs up" or "thumbs down." This process takes only about one second per rating.

Video Marketing Tips

Share Your Video On Your Socials: Twitter, Facebook, and Blog

One of the best parts of YouTube is that it's easy to share videos using the embed codes and share buttons that YouTube provides. And a solid marketing strategy involves cross posting your videos on your site, on your blog, and on your Social Media sites. According to YouTube, a link to your video in a tweet "results in 6 new youtube.com sessions on average." So once you post your videos on YouTube, post them on Twitter as well!

Leave a Video Response

You are on a video channel. How about leaving a video in the comments section instead of just leaving a written response? If you see a cover song getting thousands (or millions) of views, leave your OWN version of the song right there on the page. We call this "putting yourself in harm's way." We call it this because the video has the potential to backfire. People might be annoyed with it and leave negative comments, but there is still the potential to reach people and get more fans.

HOW TO LEAVE A VIDEO RESPONSE

STEP 1: Find a video you like.

STEP 2: Click on "Leave Video Response" under the comments section.

STEP 3: Depending on whether you have a video already created, or you want to create a video on the spot, Click "Upload Video" or "Create Video."

STEP 4: Post your video! Tell them why you love their video/channel, or whatever else you're thinking. The more you interact, the better!

Track Your Effectiveness With "Insight."

When you are logged into your channel you will see a tab on the top called "Insight." Click on it to take a deep dive into your analytics. Here you will be able to see all demographics of your viewers—male or female, where they live, etc.—and on which days your videos got the most views. You can also track where the views are coming from, which is key to determining your future marketing strategies. Looking at "Insight" will also allow you to see if your CTAs (Calls to Action) are working.

Add Your Events

You can also add your shows under the "New" Button. It's a great idea to synch your shows here for extra promotional oomph!

By mastering the tips in this chapter and following the YouTube strategies outlined in this book, you will be head and shoulders above a vast majority of artists who use the site without any guidance.

NOTES

WEEK 6: BLOGGING

Here's the first thing I'll say about blogs: Believe the hype. Content is king, and the thing that's fantastic about blogs is, they allow you to push content out—lots of it—in the form of photos, videos, or text. Therefore, blogging should become a crucial piece of your social media strategy, although it takes dedication and consistency to pull it off.

Blogging may feel like another overwhelming task to take on. Nevertheless, it's an extremely effective way to share deep insights with your fans and potential fans… and get the attention of other bloggers who can help your career.

Movie Time

Here are 2 movies to help you wrap your mind around blogging:

RSS in Plain English:

http://www.commoncraft.com/rss_plain_english

Blogs in Plain English:

http://www.commoncraft.com/blogs

GETTING PREPARED TO MANAGE BLOG READING AND COMMENTING

Create Your Google RSS Reader

Now you know exactly what this is from watching "RSS in Plain English." Setting up your RSS Reader is the perfect way to get the information you want (not only from blogs but also from other sites you frequently visit) to come to you, instead of having to check constantly to see what has been updated.

Create Your Blog Reader Profiles

Blog Reader Profiles are wonderful because they will show the blogger and the reader community that you have visited a blog even if you do not choose to comment each and every time. This leaves a trail of cyber breadcrumbs back to you, which shows others what you are interested in and where you have been.

So, if you visit a blog that has either Gravatar or Google Reader installed, a photo of you / your band logo will show up on the blog you visited. This is a great way of becoming extra memorable to bloggers. Each of these takes just a few minutes to set up.

Gravatar
http://en.gravatar.com/

Google Reader
http://www.google.com/reader

Dive In

According to the most recent statistics, there are currently over 155 million active bloggers. A few dozen people read some blogs, while some are read by millions. And as you likely know, blogs can be about any topic. The vast majority of bloggers create blogs for no financial gain whatsoever; in fact, it usually costs music bloggers money to host their files and maintain their blogs. A blog is usually a personal endeavor. Most bloggers create their blogs as an outlet where they can talk about things they are passionate about in their lives, their opinions, and the things that they like and dislike. A blog is basically an online diary.

To find blogs that are right for you won't take long. Just dive in and start reading them. The ones that resonate will jump out at you.

How to Get Reviewed on Blogs— A Step-by-Step Guide

There are 4 ways to get into the blogging world (blogosphere), some requiring a little less time or technology than others:

1. Read blogs regularly and make comments on them often.

2. Read blogs, comment a lot, AND become a blogger!
3. Hire a social media PR firm to handle blog placements for you.
4. Attend conferences and meet bloggers face to face.

I highly recommend that you get familiar with the blogging world by reading blogs and contributing by leaving comments on blogs you like about something the blogger wrote. Commenting on blogs is a very effective way to get known in the social media world.

Commenting can also get you seen by bloggers that could write about you and your music in the future. Include your signature file under your name and type out the name of your band with a link to either your website, Facebook fan page, or Twitter page. This is a subtle way of letting the blogger know you're a musician without saying, "Hey, review me!" And if the blogger likes your observations about what they wrote, they just may review you.

As a recovered traditional publicist with a background in writing press releases, announcing things, and blatantly pitching my clients, I had to start from scratch and relearn everything I thought I knew about how to promote music when I started to approach bloggers.

Bloggers are a quirky lot. I know this, because I've spent the last several years observing bloggers, interacting with bloggers through my business, and attending some of the most notable blog conferences on earth.

So, how on earth are you supposed to interrupt and say, *"Hey blogger, come write about me in your personal diary"*?

There are a few ways to do this. Here are your options.

OPTION #1: Start Your Own Blog.

The #1 piece of advice you should follow if you're trying to get known in the blogosphere is "do as they do." Start your own blog. This is a good idea for many reasons, aside from attracting other bloggers. If you don't know the big secret already: Bloggers read other bloggers' blogs! And with easy platforms like Tumblr, it's easier than ever before.

Even if you opt not to start your own blog, you need to know that having your own blog has many benefits for you as an artist:

Top 7 Reasons Every Musician Should Blog

1. Blogging is a fabulous way of keeping your fans connected to you. Blogging goes much deeper than 140 characters on Twitter or images on Flickr. Blogging also gives your fans a platform to have in depth, two-way conversations with you for the whole world to see.

2. Google loves blogs. If you set your blog up properly you'll be indexed on Google for anything and everything you write about. This means that people who were searching for other topics can find you. For instance, let's say you blog about your dog. A person who is searching for "yellow lab" could come across your blog entry, discover your music, and become a fan!

3. Blogging puts you on a level playing field with other bloggers. Bloggers read other blogs, especially those pertaining to subjects they write about—like music.

103

And a music blogger will trust you much more if you understand the whole world of blogging.

4. A blog allows you to invite your fans backstage and into your life so that they can see all sides of you... but only the sides you want to have seen. You are in control of your content. Fans can subscribe to your blog using an RSS reader and get new updates sent directly to them without having to visit your site over and over to check for new posts.

5. You can syndicate your blog posts all over the internet. ReverbNation, Facebook, Twitter, and your own website are just a few places where your blog posts can show up so people can see them and engage with you.

6. Starting a blogroll adds to your credibility with other bloggers. Add bloggers who acknowledge your blog onto your blogroll, which is a list of links to the other blogs you like or recommend, usually placed in the sidebar of your blog. In the blog world, it's critical to associate yourself with other blogs and communities of people with whom you would like to connect and with bloggers and communities that want to connect with you.

7. Blogging gets you community feedback fast. Not sure about a song lyric, a photo shoot, which night to have a gig? Ask your fans to weigh in with their opinions!

You don't have to only blog about your music; you can talk about your home life, your TV habit, your favorite foods, your day job, your fitness routine—anything! The key here is that you must post regularly and consistently. If you are in a band, having each band member contribute one post a month is a great way to keep new content flowing.

TIP: Don't over think. Just post! Do not treat this like a show or think you have to make every sentence perfect. The point of a blog is that it is an informal endeavor. Just get posting, don't stress about it, and tweak it to death. (I would, however, recommend spell check).

How to Set Up a Blog

I'm not going to go into the details about how to set them up because you can easily find guides on how to do this via Google. But the following sites are wonderful. And you can get going on them within minutes of signing up:

Blogger
http://www.Blogger.com

Wordpress
http://www.Wordpress.com

Tumblr
http://www.tumblr.com

HostBaby
http://www.hostbaby.com

Bandzoogle
http://www.bandzoogle.com

For a more advanced approach to blogging, I would suggest hiring a web designer to install a Wordpress blog right onto your website. This should not cost you more than a few hundred dollars, and your blog will then be integrated into your site. I also suggest that you add "/blog" to your personal URL. For example, my blog can be found at *http://arielpublicity.com/blog*.

TIP: If you have a website hosted by Hostbaby, they will set up your Wordpress blog for you. Contact *hostbaby@hostbaby.com*. I highly suggest this route, because then your blog will be in the same place as your website and not on a Blogger or Wordpress site. (And I also strongly advise you to build your website using the Wordpress platform. Revisit *Week 3* to remind yourself of the process.)

Measuring the Effectiveness of Your Blog with Google Analytics

As I mentioned earlier in this book when we talked about your website, Google Analytics ("GA") is an online tool that shows you how people found your site, how they explored it, and how you can enhance their visitor experience. With this information, you can monitor the effectiveness of your promotion efforts, make better informed advertising decisions, optimize your website's Google Search rank, etc. for FREE. (Be sure to revisit *Week 3* to refresh your memory about how to install and manage Google Analytics and analyze the results you see.)

OPTION #2: Become an Avid Blog Reader & Comment Back.

Option #2 is a bit less time consuming because you will not have to build and maintain your own blog, but you will still have to create personal relationships with bloggers. If you are going to go this route, I suggest you build a links page on your website, or become friends with bloggers on Facebook and feature then in your top friends. You must acknowledge other blogs so that you are still somewhat in the two-way conversation, which is critical.

TIP: If you've decided not to start your own blog, at the very least, micro-blog using Twitter. (Revisit *Week 4* for some valuable details about setting up and managing your Twitter account.)

WRITTEN EXERCISE: YOUR 10-20 BLOG TARGETS

(This one requires your trusty notebook and a computer ...or skip the notebook and just bookmark your 10-20 targets online.)

Identify 10-20 blogs where you want to be reviewed.

Once you have your own blog up and running (if you are intimidated by this part, skip it; you can still get results), the next step is to identify in which blogs you would like to be included...and then to start reading them and posting comments on them.

If you don't know how to search for blogs, here is a way to get started. Search blogs using these search engines:

http://www.blogsearch.google.com
http://www.technorati.com
http://hypem.com

Include your list of 10-20 target blogs in your blogroll. Some of the blogs you will likely find in your search are more widely read, like *Pitchfork* and *Brooklyn Vegan*. These are great targets, but I suggest you target blogs that are more likely to cover you based on what they are already writing about. Some of the most popular music blogs are indie rock centric, so if you don't play indie rock, you may not have a chance of getting included.

Search and see if any blog has already written about you. With 80 million blogs out there it's possible you've been mentioned somewhere! If you find a post that mentions you, perfect! Post a comment back thanking them for their post and **say something about their blog**. The idea is create a two-way conversation by talking about them. Use a signature file identifying yourself so they know where to visit you online.

Here's what my e-mail signature file looks like:

Ariel Hyatt
CYBER PR®
Digital Music Campaigns &
Social Media Strategies for Musicians

Ariel@ArielPublicity.com

http://www.arielpublicity.com/blog
http://www.twitter.com/cyberpr

Again, I cannot stress this enough: Your comments should never be self-promotional—not at first. They need to be about the blog, its content and / or the blogger. Comment on how you like their blog. Add feedback. Disagree, agree; but the key is participate.

When you're a blogger, you live for comments. It shows people are engaged by what you are writing. And for a blogger, this is critical.

Write down 10-20 blogs related to you and your music:

1.

2.

3.

4.

5.

6.

7.

8.

9.

10.

11.

12.

13.

14.

15.

16.

17.

18.

19.

20.

NOTES

WRITTEN EXERCISE: BLOG TOPIC LOCATOR—ARTISTS YOU KNOW / PLAY WITH

If you don't find any posts about your music, then search blogs for other artists you know and play with.

Write the names of 5-10 artists that you know and play with here that match your genre.

1.

2.

3.

4.

5.

6.

7.

8.

9.

10.

Now reach out with a personal reference and say something like:

"I just read your post about The Trews. I couldn't agree with you more. They put on a great live show. In fact we played with them just a few months ago, and I was blown away," etc.

Remember, bloggers will sense it if you're full of B.S. and just trying to get something by commenting. So let your intention be connection, not promotion.

Say something very specific about their blog post and then add your own detailed comments. Keep in mind that blogs are all about adding to the community, so be a contribution.

TIP: Don't ask for a review on your first contact with a blogger—just make an observation about them and comment on what they are writing. There will be plenty of time to make yourself known later—this is a process that takes some time.

Don't forget that bloggers are people too, and all PR is about connecting personally. If you do not handle this tactfully, the blogger will sense that you are just trying to get something.

WRITTEN EXERCISE: BLOG TOPIC LOCATOR—SEARCH BY SOUND ALIKE & COMPARISON

Another way to identify blogs that are likely to write about you is to search for blog posts about bands or artists that sound like you. If you're always getting compared to a certain band or artist, find out who is blogging about them. They could be a good blog to follow, read and comment on.

TIP: Stay away from the huge names like Bob Dylan and search for more niche artists that are comparable to you.

After Your Search

Now that you've researched and found 10-20 blogs on which you want to be mentioned or reviewed, blogs by other musicians you know, blogs that have already written about you, and blogs that have written about music similar to yours, **go visit these blogs and take a peek.**

Is this the kind of blog that would write about you? If so, add this blog to your RSS reader and return to it and comment often. Add this blog to your blogroll, so that the blogger can see that you are visiting often.

Remember, in order to stand out you have to regularly post comments on other people's blogs before ever making your first pitch. After weeks of tracking and posting comments, you can write a simple "hello" to the blogger, mention that you have a blog and you also have music you'd like them to check out.

TIP: In order to become sticky you will have to post comments on other people's blogs regularly and get to be known by the blogger before you make your first pitch.

After you get your first review, remember to link back to your blog and thank the blogger.

As I said before, bloggers read other bloggers' blogs. Soon, you will begin to spread around the net.

OPTION #3: Hire a Social Media PR Firm to Handle Blog Placements For You.

I suggest that you do your research thoroughly and make sure you are very clear what it is you want before you go down this path.

I wrote a guide called "The Musicians Guide To Choosing The Perfect Publicist" which is included in *Week 9* of this book. Read it before you hire someone!

OPTION #4: Attend Conferences and Meetups and Meet Bloggers Face to Face.

This is a great way to get into the blogging community. Here are a few I suggest:

SXSW Interactive
http://www.SXSW.com

Mid-March in Austin, TX.

BlogHer
http://www.blogher.com/conferences

August in San Diego, CA.

BlogWorld & New Media Expo
http://www.blogworldexpo.com

November in Los Angeles, CA

Can't travel ? That's okay.

Meetup
http://www.meetup.com

There are tons of bloggers meeting up for drinks in every city and state in the US and abroad, so log in and join a group. I randomly joined the podcasting NYC group and out of it have met some of my closest allies in the business. Meetups are highly recommended and FREE!

NOTES

WEEK 7: YOUR NEWSLETTER

Think of yourself as a commodity, and your fan as a customer.

This week's lesson could mean the difference between you making a little money off of your music vs. you making A LOT of money.

A recent study conducted by Top Spin Media—a well-known music marketing platform—has shown that 30% of its users' overall revenue was generated through their newsletters. Fans have a tendency to buy when they see a clear "Call to Action" in a newsletter. The sample in the data is comprised of a cross section of campaigns monitored, featuring many artists from different genres.

To make a long story short, in the online world, e-mail is still king when it comes to generating revenue, specifically for musicians. You make relationships with fans on your social networks and turn these fans into customers with your newsletter.

Before we dive in: You may be freaking out here a bit. In your mind your fans are not customers. Your fans don't "buy" from you, and you do not consider them in that light. And I totally understand this. But, I am asking you to take off your artist hat for a minute and put on your business hat. In order to be successful, you must think about your fans as customers.

All of the current news surrounding the music business is bad news. Record industry veterans are getting laid off left and right, and CD sales continue to drop as consumers get free music online. The old music business is still stuck in the same old pattern: sell one CD each to a million people (or many millions) and SUCCESS! This strategy is all about selling many copies of **limited items:** CDs; downloads; etc.

It's no longer sufficient to have only CDs and downloadable tracks for sale, because in your customer's mind there is little to no value attached to CDs and downloads. And working to your disadvantage is that free downloads and streams are readily available everywhere online.

This is an exciting time to come up with some alternatives and create some offerings for your core fan base that will, in the long run, make you a lot more money. It's time to break the mold and create something that is more sustainable for you as an artist.

The new paradigm should be a 2-pronged approach:

1. Sell *MANY items* to a smaller group of your core fans who know, love and trust you and want to come back to you and to your brand many times for more.

2. Create a sense of belonging and community around your music. By doing this, your fans will feel like they are members of a club and not just buying a one-time thing.

How will you achieve this?

It will take some time and strategy.

"1,000 True Fans"

Before you read the rest of this chapter, I highly recommend you read "1,000 True Fans:" *http://bit.ly/1000TrueFans*. It's one of the most important articles written about making money in today's swiftly-shifting new music business. It is mentioned by the experts at every key music conference and referenced in almost all forward-thinking conversations about today's new music business.

Ariel's "In Defense of 1,000 True Fans"

I was so taken with the philosophy behind "1,000 True Fans" because it outlines the paradigm that I have been working in for my entire career in the music business. So I set out to demonstrate the theory by interviewing several artists who have been proving it in many different ways.

So, I created a blog series called "In Defense of 1,000 True Fans." It now has 11 installments featuring artists who are utilizing this theory with many different tools—from streaming house concerts, to film and TV placements—and making full-time livings off relatively small but supportive fan bases.

You can access it here:

http://arielpublicity.com/category/blog/1000-true-fans/

The First Step: Build Rapport with Your Email List

This comes down to communicating regularly and consistently with your fan base and then—when the time is right—asking them for money.

I have seen it countless times: Artists totally misuse their e-mail lists by only reaching out to their fans when they have something to sell them (a show, a new release, etc.). But they never reach out to their fans for other reasons (to share news, say, "hi," ask their opinions, invite them out for a drink, and get fans more involved with them).

Many artists I work with argue with me about this point and say that their fans get angry with them if they communicate with their lists too much.

If someone does not want to receive communications from you, that's okay. They can and should remove themselves from your list. People who want to be removed from your list probably won't buy from you anyway, so remove them with joy, and get on with bonding with the core fan base that really wants to hear from you.

WRITTEN EXERCISE: BRAINSTORMING—CREATING RAPPORT

Here are some ideas about how to improve your monthly newsletters. Start to think about ways to get fans to open and read your e-mails, and why they look forward to receiving them.

Answer The Following Questions:

Who Are Your Fans?

» Are they male or female?

» Are they singles or couples?

» How old are they?

» How much money do they make on average?

What Do They Like To Do?

» Is there an activity/hobby they like?

> Skiing?

> Surfing?

> Hiking with their dogs?

> Wine tasting?

» When they are not seeing live music, what do they do?

> Go to movies?

> Eat at restaurants?

> Attend parties?

» If you were hanging out with a cross-section of them at a party, what would they be talking about?

> Their families/kids?

> Their classes in school?

> What else?

Where Do They Hang Out?

» Bars?

» Restaurants?

» Dance clubs?

» Yoga class?

» Gym?

» Skate park?

» Mommy groups?

» The mall?

» Coffee shop?

» High school?

» College?

» Other?

» Do they go on vacation?

> Is it hot or cold?

> Are they with family?

> Do they travel in groups?

On Which Websites Do They Congregate?

» Facebook?

» LinkedIn?

» Flickr?

» Google+?

» Blogs?

» Twitter?

» Other?

Other Questions:

» Do they like blogs, podcasts or other new media outlets, or are computers intimidating to them?

» Which magazines or books do they read?

» Do they like sports? Which ones?

» Do they meet or spend time together outside of your shows?

Sum it Up

Now look over your answers, go back and circle the responses that have a consistent theme or a few themes. Write down your observations. You will use this information while you write your newsletter.

Choose Some Themes

If they are your fans, then you will share a lot of the same hobbies and traits with them. What could you add to your monthly / bi-monthly newsletter that would engage them, based on what you have brainstormed?

Choosing a Newsletter Provider

There are many reputable newsletter platforms available. We have had very positive experiences with the ones mentioned below. These different descriptions will help you choose which provider will be best for you.

FanBridge—*http://bit.ly/FanBridgeInfo*

If you want more control over the HTML design, the contact list itself, etc., we recommend FanBridge. It's very easy to import your existing contacts using an Excel file. They also make it possible to set up a "Fan Incentive" where fans can trade you their e-mail addresses in exchange for music (e.g. an MP3, which is a phenomenal way to accumulate contacts). It is also possible to update all your statuses for FanBridge, Facebook, and Twitter from the FanBridge dashboard.

Nimbit—*http://bit.ly/NimbitInfo*

If you are looking for a one-stop shop for both your newsletter and your online commerce, Nimbit is the place. If you are ready to set storefronts on your homepage or on Facebook, we would recommend looking into what they have to offer. Do be aware that as of this writing, they take a 20% cut of all transactions through their storefronts (fees of this type are fairly common).

ReverbNation—*http://bit.ly/FanReachInfo*

If you are already using ReverbNation, there is no reason to leave. They have a great service when it comes to newsletter management. They also have great widgets that may appeal to you. You can use it for full integration.

Creating an Engaging Newsletter—The 3 G'S: Greeting, Guts, & Getting

At the very top of the newsletter, sum up what is about to follow so people know what is coming in your newsletter.

PART 1. Greeting—Make it Personal

Provide an introduction of yourself and some personal information. Share something non-music related here. This should be a wrap-up of what you have been up to such as a vacation, family time, what you are reading or listening to, TV and movies you are watching and why you liked them, etc. Post photos of these personal touches on Flickr, Facebook, your homepage, etc.

PART 2. Guts—The Meat of Your Newsletter

This is the meat of the newsletter, or what you as an artist, or the whole band have/has been up to. Are you in the studio? On the road? Writing new tracks?

Remember, people love and connect to stories, so **tell stories**. And don't be afraid to be engaging and real.

PART 3. Getting—Put Readers into Action

This is the part of the newsletter that gets your fans to take action on your part.

Examples of Calls to Action for Community Building
(Do these **before** you provide any Calls to Action for money.)

Invite them to ...

» Follow you on Twitter.

» "Like" your Facebook Fan Page.

» Listen to a new track on your Facebook Fan Page.

» Vote for you in an online contest you might be in.

» Comment on your blog.

» Review you on iTunes, Amazon or CD Baby.

» Hang out with you at a bar, club, coffee house, another person's show, etc. (This is great for bonding with them on another level.)

» Watch a video of you on YouTube and subscribe to your YouTube channel.

» Fill out a survey you send them or enter a contest.

» Enjoy a free download of one of your songs.
(A special gift makes you memorable!)

TIP: There should only be *one* "Get" (call to action) per newsletter. Fans will get confused and overwhelmed if you include more than one.

The Subject Line

Keep your subject line short and sweet—no more than 55 characters!

Studies show that including the reader's first name in the subject line grabs their attention and increases your open rate (the amount of people that open your e-mail). Most newsletter management programs can easily insert first names right into the subject line. Please consult with yours on how to do so.

Here are some captivating phrases that work:

» "Hey (First Name), Join me for/at ..."

» "Hey (First Name), Find out how ..."

» "(First Name), did you know that ..."

Subject lines like the ones above pique the reader's curiosity.

Surveys: How to Ask Your Fans What They Want

Before you assume what it is your fans would like from you, I suggest that you conduct a free survey and ask them!

Survey Monkey is a wonderful site where you can create a FREE survey of up to 10 questions and send it around to your list for feedback. If you want to do a complete, in-depth survey, it's only $24.99 per month. *http://www.surveymonkey.com*

If you're looking for an even less expensive option, Poll Daddy is another great resource for polls and surveys (It's free!): *http://polldaddy.com*

The most successful marketers **always** test the waters before they release anything. A survey can help you create as a brand and launch a product line that caters directly to your fans. After all, it is your fans who will give you money and support your creative work.

There are many things to consider when you look at it in this light:

» What is your product line? Do you only sell CDs? Do you have merch? A fan club? A line of products that you can sell to your fans?

127

» Do you have a real fan base/e-mail list to sell these things to? I consider a real fan base a **minimum** of 500, but between 5,000-10,000 is a great goal number to work towards.

» Have you asked your fans what they want, what they are willing to buy, and how much they are willing to spend?

» Have you ever let your fans know they can invite you to play a house or school concert, a backyard party, or a corporate event? (You can do this by simply mentioning that you are available for private events in your newsletter.)

» Do you have another talent that your fans don't know about? Do you paint? Do you write, etc.?

» Can you create some sort of monthly continuum program that your fans might pay a monthly premium for? How about a "Live Track of the Month" club or a special new song you are working on? Would your fans pay $2 a month for that? If you think so, that's $24 per fan, and that adds up.

So, To Recap:

Build your e-mail list! Every day, think about who you can add to your list.

When your list gets to be at least 500 strong, create a survey that asks them what they would like from you. Create products and fan clubs and house concerts to satisfy your fans and generate more money!

Examples of Calls to Action for Money
(once you've developed rapport):

» Invite them to an upcoming show.

» Invite them to buy your music on iTunes or CDBaby—one track or a whole album.

» Sell a merch item—a hat, a t-shirt, etc.

» Let them know you play backyard BBQs and private parties; have them e-mail you if they are interested (money maker #1).

» Record personalized songs upon request (money maker #2).

WRITTEN EXERCISE: WRITE DOWN SOME IDEAS FOR YOUR NEXT NEWSLETTER

Now go back through the first part of this Week or use the responses from your "Creating E-mail Rapport" survey and find some themes and topics that your fans will like. List them here.

1.

2.

3.

4.

5.

6.

You just wrote 6; that's 6 months worth of newsletter themes.

Building Your Mailing List

I believe your e-mail newsletter list is your most valuable asset and the most critical aspect of your career in the rapidly-changing music business.

Building Your Fan Base = Building Your E-mail List
The Size of Your E-mail List = The Size of Your Income

So, how big is yours?

What artists try to tell me is they don't play many (or any) gigs, and therefore they say that there is no need to create a newsletter.

The truth is: most of the artists that I work with don't have any shows to promote. If you want to be an artist (whether you play live or not) you still need to get your music and your message out. To do this, you must communicate something to your fans **regularly** and **consistently**.

If you disappear from the hearts and minds of your fans for several months, they will not know where you've been, and they will disengage. You also want to bear in mind that if you only e-mail your fans when you have a show, or a new CD to sell them, it totally screams, "Hey fan, I want your money!"

You just show up out of nowhere and say, "I know you had no idea where I've been for the last six months, but here, buy something now!" Because people hate being sold to, they will naturally resist you. People do, however, love to belong and to participate actively in communities, so if you can make them feel like they belong, you will be well on your way.

131

6 Tips For Getting More Fans Onto Your Newsletter List

1. Add Friends & Family

   Mine through your inbox and outbox. We all have them: huge inboxes stuffed with e-mail from people who you're communicating with. Are they already on your e-mail list? If not, e-mail each of them and ask: "Is it okay for me to add you to my newsletter list?" Be sure to offer a free MP3, and if they say yes, add them!

   TIP: Never ever add someone without getting permission first, even if it's a friend, because that's considered SPAM.

   Send a simple e-mail that says something like this:

   *Dear [**NAME**],*

   I was just going through my in-box and I came across our last e-mail. *(**Say something personal that connects you to this person here—how you met, who you know in common, the last event you attended etc.**)*

   Would it be okay if I add you to my monthly / bimonthly e-mail list? I would love to keep you in the loop about what I am up to as an artist and from time to time I give away free music too!

   Please let me know if it's okay with you.

   I will never give your e-mail address to anyone else, and you can opt out of my list at any time.

   Thanks,
   Signature File

2. Create a Separate In-box for Potential
   E-Mail Sign-ups

   Name it—"Potential Newsletter Reader." And
   throughout the week when you get an e-mail from
   someone who you think would make a nice addition to the list, simply move it into that specific box.
   Then, when it's time for your scheduled hour, sit
   down and build your list.

3. Make It Irresistable—Give Away A Free,
   Exclusive MP3 or Video

   Let's face it, people are motivated by self interest.
   Remember, when they come onto your website, they
   are asking the "What's In It For Me?" question in
   their heads.

   Give them a bribe of a free track to "incentivize"
   them! Add a box to your website that says, "Sign up
   to my monthly newsletter and receive an exclusive
   track from my newest album (or an exclusive live
   track or video)."

   TIP: Do not have this same track available on your
   Facebook fan page. Make it exclusive to your site only.
   But DO advertise it on your social networking sites!

4. List Trade With Another Band

   Once you have a sizeable e-mail list, you can approach other bands that you play with or whose
   music is similar to yours (or maybe they're from
   your hometown or share some other common interest), and you can ask them to write an endorsement
   e-mail saying:

133

Hey, if you like us, you'll like our friends!

Then they can send that endorsement out with a request for joining your e-mail list and you can, in turn, do the same for them. Always have a free MP3 as an incentive.

When you do a list trade with another band, always make sure that your music is very well described in a couple of sentences. Talk about what you sound like, who you get compared to, etc., so your potential fans will know what to expect.

If you can, take them directly to a page where they can get a free MP3 that's streaming the moment they sign up so they can check you out.

5. Get Mobile—Start A Text Message List

Sending a text message to your fans is original and stands out (e-mails tend not to stand out).

I recommend using a free service to capture mobile/cellular phone numbers called Broadtexter. It's free and you can add their widget to your website, Facebook Fan Page, Myspace page, etc.
http://www.broadtexter.com

TIP: Before you start playing a gig, when you ask fans to switch off their cell phones, ask them first to text you their information. Then you build a cell phone directory list, and you can SMS people directly to their cell phones the next time you're coming through town. This is a totally unique and original way of communicating on people's cellular phones and will get you noticed.

Amanda Palmer did this and got hundreds of new fans on to her list each night by giving out her tour manager's cell phone number. His cell phone was used as a list builder.

6. Schedule a Set Time Each Week for List Building

Create a time at least once a week to sit down and actively add to your e-mail list. You will be amazed at how many people you meet and come into contact with who you do not add to your list because it slipped your mind. But with some focus, you can become a list-building animal.

When I started regularly communicating with the fans on my fan list at Ariel Publicity, magic started happening. My articles started getting picked up and reprinted online. People started leaving me nice messages and saying, "Thank you for your newsletter. Your advice made an impact."

I even hosted my first all-day workshop that came directly from people on my newsletter list and it sold out so fast I had to add a second session!

Why?

Because I sent e-mails regularly and consistently, and people began to trust me and like what I had to say—and then I asked them for money.

In other words, I made money by just **communicating and asking**.

Studies prove that people buy from people they like and trust, and there is no better way to earning people's trust than by communicating with them on a regular basis. And you should talk about something personal and fun or unique about yourself offstage that your fans may not know. So, go out there and build your e-mail list.

Live Show Bonus: Do a Giveaway / Raffle at Every Show

When you are playing a show, hold up a CD or a t-shirt on stage and announce you are doing a free give-away and a raffle. Have a friend sweep through the venue with a hat, and have everyone drop their business cards into the hat. When the hat reaches the stage, pull a random business card out and do a give-away. If your fans don't have business cards, use note cards they can write on, or use a clipboard.

Have the winner come up to the stage and hold up the CD to show the audience. This is giving yourself and your product a plug in front of everyone and is great subliminal marketing. Then, mention to the crowd that you're going to add everyone in the hat to your e-mail list. You've just collected a ton of new e-mail names and addresses that you definitely would not have captured.

So to summarize…

Your Main Goal is: *Grow Your List.*

EXERCISE: 6 STEPS TO JUMP-START YOUR MAILING LIST BUILDING RIGHT NOW!

1. Make dates with yourself: Look at your calendar for the next month (and, if you can, for the next 3–6 months) and schedule some time—at least 60–90 minutes—where you will sit down and focus only on building your e-mail list.

2. Create a list of bands/artists who you play with or are friendly with, who could do a list trade or an endorsement with you. List them here:

3. Draft a "form e-mail" that you keep in a folder on your computer that you can send around to potential list candidates to get their permission. (There is one on page 132; simply use it as a backbone and modify it to suit your needs.)

4. Visit these 3 mobile fan list management sites and see which one may work for you: *http://www.broadtexter.com, http://www.mozes.com, http://www.Texting.ly.*

5. Contact your web designer and have him add a "bribe," or a free and exclusive, downloadable MP3 to your homepage immediately, so you can capture more people who visit your site.

6. Go to *http://bit.ly/reverbfreebribe* and grab the "Exclusive Downloads" widget (there are many other wonderful widgets available here as well). Add these widgets to your PledgeMusic page, your Facebook Fan Page and to all your pages on social Media sites to capture more signups.

NOTES

WEEK 8: CREATING A CONTINUUM PROGRAM

Getting Your Fans To Buy From You Over and Over Again

This week deals with Continuum Programs, which are the #1 way that marketers and successful business owners make money.

Before we move ahead, let's recap what you have already accomplished and implemented:

» Your newsletter is going out at least once or twice a month.

» You are posting your newsletter content on Facebook, Twitter, and blogs.

» Your e-mail list is steadily growing.

» You are setting aside at least 1 hour, once per week to build your e-mail list.

» You have surveyed your core fans and you know what it is that they want, or you have at least identified new insights about them.

Now, it's time to start thinking about creating your Continuum Program. This will be the system you use to get your fans to buy from you on a regular basis.

The concept is simple: Entice your fans so they will give you money on a consistent basis. But keep in mind, you can only do this after they have begun to engage with you and after they trust you. Remember the Columbia Records program from back in the day? Their concept was simple: Give the music-lover customer a lot of value (12 cassettes for $1); then offer them albums they will like based on their tastes for a monthly premium.

With that in mind, what can you offer your fans on an ongoing basis that will get them to buy?

Note that this does not have to be an every-single-month buy: It can be 4 times per year. The concept here is consistency! And the following marketing funnel will give you a great system for organizing it all.

The Funnel—A Basic Marketing Principle for Making Money

The marketing funnel is the way that smart businesses make money. The principle is simple to grasp and makes sense to musicians because so many musicians are already implementing the top few tiers of the funnel.

At the very opening (to get fans into the funnel) you make a free offer that fans can't refuse, in exchange for their e-mail addresses. An exclusive MP3 or a video are both really effective freebies / incentives.

Once the fan is in your funnel, and you are sending them regular communications, you can ask them to pay for something: a download for 99 cents, a ticket to a show, or perhaps a full album.

The idea of the funnel is the more loyal, engaged, and interested your fan becomes, the more money he will be willing to spend on you as he moves down the funnel.

As the funnel gets smaller—at the bottom—you want to add more expensive items to it.

The concept behind this strategy is that the most die-hard and engaged fans who love you the most will buy many things from you, and hopefully everything you have to offer! And keep in mind, there are a few people on everyone's list that will want expensive offers.

Here is what a funnel looks like:

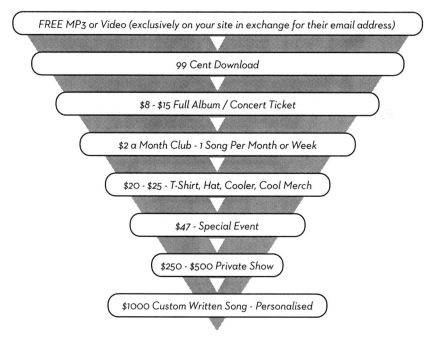

FREE MP3 or Video (exclusively on your site in exchange for their email address)

99 Cent Download

$8 - $15 Full Album / Concert Ticket

$2 a Month Club - 1 Song Per Month or Week

$20 - $25 - T-Shirt, Hat, Cooler, Cool Merch

$47 - Special Event

$250 - $500 Private Show

$1000 Custom Written Song - Personalised

EXERCISE: CREATING YOUR FUNNEL

Here is a blank funnel for you to fill in. (Actually I provided three blank funnels, because over the course of the next few weeks or months they may change as you create new ideas and products to sell.)

Fill One in:

Don't worry if you don't already have some of the things you will be adding to the funnel...just **write**!

Date:

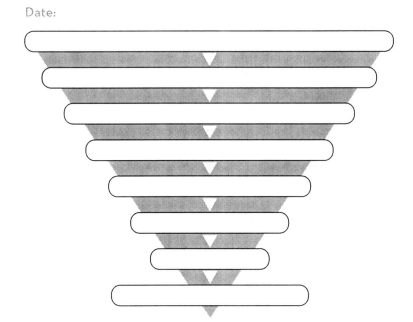

Date:

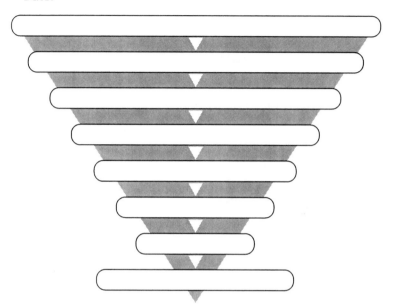

Date:

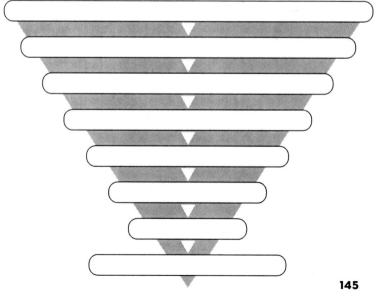

Following are some ideas for a range of expensive things for your funnel.

Continuum Program Ideas

1. Monthly Fan Club

    Record a unique track or video once a month and charge your fans a small fee to join the club ($2-$3 a month).

2. Special Events with the Band Club

    Create a fan club that hosts 4-6 special events a year. Not all of them have to be you performing. You can get creative. Have a wine tasting, a dessert party, or a pub crawl. Get local businesses involved by holding these events on a slow night, like a Monday, or during a down month for the business. (January can be slow for a lot of restaurants.)

3. Artist Critique / Feedback

    Invite your biggest fans to come hear new songs you've written. Play them in an acoustic setting around a big circle. Give them cards and let them vote on the songs they like. This makes your fans feel extra included because they can help you choose what you will be releasing next.

4. Private Gigs

    You can play a dinner party or a backyard BBQ that's private-invite only. You could arrange these a few times per year. Announce the fact that you are available to play private gigs in your newsletter. And if you have a P.A., you can explain that you are ready to show up and play!

5. Clothing / Merch Item of the Month Club

I've seen a few bands do a t-shirt of the month club. It could also be a ski hat in February and a tank top in August. Could you create a fun item of the month club for fans?

6. An Event for Each Season

How about a concert for each season? This would be a great way to get fans to pay 4 times per year. Hold a quarterly concert with a theme, such as Halloween, Valentine's Day, Summer Solstice, April Fools, or Winter Wonderland. Make it a special event so they can dress up or dress down.

7. Annual Camping Festival

I worked with a band called *ekoostik hookah* for many years, and they hold a camping festival twice per year in their home state of Ohio. These festivals attracted thousands of fans from across the whole state, who paid big bucks to spend Labor Day and Memorial Day with the band and see them play with other artists. *moe* also does this with their annual *moedown* festival. These events make them tens of thousands of dollars. And their fans look forward to the camaraderie.

8. Be the Belle of the Ball

There's a band in New York City called *Valeze* that built a cult following by decorating the venues each time they played with streamers and balloons. They would have a theme like "circus" or "disco," and everybody would get decked out and attend the shows, which became great parties because they were truly special events.

147

9. Charity Affiliation

Affiliate with a charity and donate a portion of your event proceeds to that chosen charity. If you reach out to the charity and tell them you are holding an event in their honor, they may be willing to partner with you and help you promote your special event. Align with a local charity in your hometown to strengthen your local ties.

10. Private VIP Fan Website

Create a special website that only your fans can access. On it, offer them special things like wallpapers, screen savers, and other bonus gifts. You could also create a special paid podcast, once per month, where you not only play your own music but also recommend, interview, and play other artists your fans might like.

How much could you charge for any or all of these ideas?

Do The Math!

If you charge just 200 fans $5 per month to be in your top-tier fan club with exclusive offers and membership just for them, that equals $12,000 a year in extra income. And you can set it up so that PayPal puts that money directly into your bank account on a monthly basis.

If you charge 1,000 fans $2 a month to be in your song of the week/month club, that's $24,000 a year!

EXERCISE: CONTINUUM PROGRAM IDEA GENERATION

Go over the 10 ideas that I outlined above and circle one or two that could work for you and your music and fans.

Write down 3 ideas that cater to your fans that you could introduce within the next 3 months as an added way to produce income:

1.

2.

3.

WRITTEN EXERCISE: COMPLETING YOUR FUNNEL

Now write down the things you will need to do in order to get the funnel complete.

For example:

» Order t-shirts.

» Record a song per week / month.

» Create an "extra video content for free" offer.

» Research where to have a dinner party/costume ball.

» Select a charity with which you feel it is right for you to align.

6 Ideas For Building Your Funnel

1.

2.

3.

4.

5.

6.

Fan Funding

Building a funnel is crucial to long-term success. But what if you need to get an infusion of cash to make a large project come to life?

Fan funding—also called "crowd funding"—is a way for artists to approach the music industry and their fans by creating a unique experience that offers direct-to-fan benefits.

In recent years, fan funding has been a process instrumental to helping artists find a single solution to satisfy the issues of the lack of funding available from labels as well an increased desire for attention and empowerment from fans. Not only has fan funding become a reliable alternative for artists who have an existing fan base, but it also offers more value to fans than ever before through a system of incentives and updates.

As you have learned in this book, regular use of Social Media has built up a new-found desire among fans for artists to share their world in its entirety. And today's fans crave attention. For an artist in today's music industry to thrive, the fans must be given what they want: More of the artist, all the time.

Here are my 4 favorite platforms to explore if you are interested in launching a fan funding initiative (in alphabetical order). Each of these sites takes a different percentage and has different rules about keeping the money if you only partially fund your project (a great argument!) as opposed to only if you get the full 100 percent. And a few of these sites let you offer the donations as a tax write-off. Make sure you do your research before choosing a site, as rules for use can vary significantly across platforms and continue to change as fan funding evolves.

Indie GoGo—*http://www.indiegogo.com*
Kickstarter—*http://www.kickstarter.com*
Pledge Music—*http://www.pledgemusic.com*
Rockethub—*http://rockethub.com*

Before you embark on a fan funding campaign...

Ask yourself how many true fans you actually have—fans that would part with money to support you. Are there 50, are there 100, are there 1,000? How do you communicate with these fans? Do you have their e-mail addresses, their physical addresses? Are these people that you see frequently and often, or people that you are in some sort of contact with on Social Media websites? Understand that there is a distinct difference between a true fan that you know and is willing to part with money to support you, and a fan that may just be following you on a social networking platform like Facebook or Twitter. The idea here is to gather them up and make a good assessment of how many and how much money you think each one would be willing to part with to support you on your journey.

The Cart Before The Horse—Knowing Your Limits

A word of caution: Know your limits. In the world of fan funding, creating a goal like "$15,000" may feel possible. But ask yourself, "How much did I earn in the past 12 months from my music, and what would a reasonable goal be to reach for?" If you sold $500 worth of music in 2010, then a goal of $1,000 (twice what you made the year before) may be smart, instead of setting yourself up for failure and shooting for a massive number.

Asking: The Necessary Evil, a.k.a. the Reality of Asking your Fans for Money

The following are two very real takes on the way the crowd-funding experience makes you feel.

Spin magazine ran an article in July 2010 about fan funding, and Artist Momus (who successfully launched a crowd-funded campaign) was quoted as saying, "I felt like a carnival barker."

Jill Sobule, who has been heavily covered all over the blogosphere and in the media about her fan funding said, "At times I felt too much like a business person."

It's much easier to blame uncomfortable feelings like the ones described above on the record label, the radio promoter, the fact that your manager sucked, or whatever other excuse you want to insert here.

It's not about the money, it's about the journey.

A common misconception of the fan funding process is that it is a glorified pre-order for an upcoming album, and understandably so. Similar to a pre-order, fan funding has artists reaching out to fans to give money up front, with the understanding that they will receive the music once it is released. The two are also similar because either technique requires an existing fan base in order to work.

However, this is really where the comparison ends.

A pre-order is about money. It is a process that revolves around a finished product. A fan funding campaign, however, is not at all about the money, nor does it revolve around the finished product. The focal point of any successful fan funding campaign is the journey and process of making the final product. In some cases, the journey is through the artist's process of writing and recording. In other cases, the journey could be to finish mastering or even just properly distribute a new album. Every journey is different, and that's because of how personal the experience of creating music is.

The key here is taking your fans on this journey with you—so it doesn't end as it becomes a journey for you all. The fan funding campaign is really just the beginning of a life-long journey between artist and fan base. Once a fan buys into the experience, it becomes more than a voyeuristic 'journey to make an album', but rather it becomes about the fan's own journey as a member of a community.

It has to be a desirable experience for the fans; it's about them.

A successful fan funding campaign is a personal experience for both artist and the artist's fan base. Sure, the artist must hit the set campaign goal in order for it to be a success for them. But what about the fans? The only way an artist can actually achieve any goal is if they help the fans achieve their goals first. Once the fans are satisfied and on board, they will then help the artist achieve any goals under the sun.

In order for a fan funding campaign to be a success for the fans, it must offer additional value and establish an emotional connection with the artist that is unattainable anywhere else. So, when designing and preparing a fan funding campaign, the primary focus must be to create a desirable experience for the fans.

What Happens if You Fail?

"Success is the ability to go from one failure to another with no loss of enthusiasm."

Sir Winston Churchill

NOTES

WEEK 9: THE REAL WORLD

Real-life Networking Tips

How to Get People on Your Mailing List In Person

A major lesson you have been getting out of this book so far is the importance of getting people on your e-mail list.

Here are some real-life "Networking 101" tips that I learned from sales and networking guru Larry Sharpe. Larry is such a master at networking that people literally line up to talk to him at parties and events.

There Are Three Reasons Why We Network:

1. To find a direct target / customer / fan. For example, a fan that will buy tickets, music, or merch and

support you. (But first you need to get them on your e-mail list and build rapport.)

2. To gain a sphere of influence, and therefore a source for referrals (i.e. people who like the people that know and support your music/brand/band).

3. As a resource for you and your fans.

When you go into any networking / social situation...

The biggest goal of networking is, "Be memorable." How do you do that?

It's simple: The more **they** talk, the more memorable **you** are.

On First Contact

When you meet people, first ask a question about **them**. So, for example, if you are approaching someone at a wedding, you could say, "What brought you here today? How did you meet the bride?" Get them talking.

Never walk up to someone and say: "Hi, I'm David." That makes it all about **you**. Instead, you want to say something like, "So, Nancy, what do you do?" Or, "Are you having a good time?" Or, "What brings you here today?" Then, it's all about **them**.

Business Cards

If you don't have one already and are above the age of 18, **get a business card now**! You have no excuse; they are free. Go here:

http://www.VistaPrint.com

Or design your own and print them:
http://www.jakprints.com

TIP: Put one sentence about your music (your "pitch"), and the instrument you play on your card. A card with just a name and an address is totally unmemorable!

TIP: Put a photo of yourself or your band logo on the card to add even more branding and recognition. Make sure you list your e-mail, website, and links. I love Moo Cards:

http://bit.ly/MiniMooCards

Don't worry about giving out your card. Focus on getting THEIR cards. Never give your card out unless someone asks for it. If you present someone with a card, you are selling. (And as mentioned before, people hate selling.) If someone asks for your card, they are buying. (And people actually love buying.)

What Next?

After getting people to talk about themselves a little bit and maybe exchanging business cards, follow these ABCs when you go to a party, wedding, or any social situation:

A. Know What to Ask For

For example:

» A private gig
» A student to teach lessons to
» A place to rehearse

...and of course, you can always ask for an e-mail address if you do not have any other specific goal that day.

B. Be a Gatherer

This means that whenever you are in any social situation, you should be gathering as much information as possible about each person: interesting tidbits about them; what they like; who they know; where they go; etc.

TIP: For this, don't think about yourself! Think, "How can I be helpful to this person that I'm talking to?" Let go of your story and your pitch and let others talk all about themselves.

C. Follow Up

After you get home, and it's time to follow up, never send your marketing pitch or talk about your business in the initial e-mail. Get people to respond to your follow-up.

Say something very simple without a pitch:

> "Dear Leslie, It was nice to meet you. Weren't those little pigs in blankets delicious?"

Then close the e-mail with your name and signature file that has your links to your site, Facebook, Twitter, etc. (For an example, see mine on page 108.)

If they respond, then you can begin to establish rapport and eventually pitch them. So, remember, the first follow-up should always be friendly and positive and NOT business-oriented!

Be a Shark in a Sea of Tuna.

When networking, don't think about your industry. If you are trying to grow your business (and you should always be trying to grow your business), it's helpful to go to the places that are the exact opposite of your industry.

So, as a musician, you would go and network with a bunch of other musicians if you were looking for more people to play with or to tap into a community of musicians. However, this is probably not going to make you money.

If you go to, say, a bridal convention, and you meet a whole bunch of people who are planning weddings, and you introduce yourself as a musician, you might get some really good gigs.

Conduct Your Initial Follow-Up on the Phone.

You can say something like, *"Hey, Larry. Laura asked me to give you a call. This is Ariel."* Use only your first name. Never say, *"Hi, my name is Ariel,"* because then people will think of you as a stranger (you would never call your mom and say: *"Hi, my name is Ariel."* It's too formal).

So, just say: *"I'm Ariel,"* or *"This is Ariel,"* and then carry on with your conversation.

Words / phrases never (ever) to say:

» *"I'm just..."*
» *"I'm not looking to sell you anything..."*
» *"I'm not looking for connections..."*

Don't use these phrases to try to put another person at ease, because that person will immediately think the opposite. The brain doesn't register "I'm just..."

How to Position Yourself When It's Your Turn to Talk

When they are finally engaged with you (after they have talked about themselves) and you are ready to make your pitch, talk about what other people say about you, instead of pitching yourself.

Why? Because people always believe what other people say about you more than they believe you saying it about yourself!

So, you could say something like: "People say my music sounds like Bob Dylan crossed with a touch of The Beatles." Or, "My voice gets compared to Annie Lennox."

These types of statements will register very well.

EXERCISE: MENTALLY PREPARING FOR WHAT YOU WANT BEFORE YOU GO OUT

Okay, you are ready to go to a party, a wedding, an event for a friend, etc.

This exercise takes 5 minutes.

1. Go to a quiet place.
2. Take a deep breath.
3. Focus on what it is you would like today, this week, this month to move your musical career forward.
4. If you need to, write down the one or two things you would like.
5. The default thing you can always ask for is a business card so you can grow your e-mail list.
6. Keep that thing in mind when you walk out the door.

Do you really want it?

Before you walk in the room, touch your head and repeat to yourself the exact thing/things that you want.

Traditional PR—An Overview

I believe it is critical to understand the basics of publicity in order to advance your career. In this section, I will go over how to write a standard press release—which you may need to do from time to time when you need to approach the traditional media. And I will provide a full overview of traditional PR and how to do it. You may never want to or have to, but I think it's important to understand the full scope of how PR works so if you ever hire or manage a publicist you will understand the structure and be able to oversee her work to make sure that she is serving you well.

I often go on and on about how I personally abandoned "traditional" PR. But it still has its place and can produce fruitful results when handled properly. I encourage all artists to include it as part of their outreach strategy.

8 Simple Steps **to Formatting a Proper Press Release**

A press release should be one page only and on letterhead. (I know fewer and fewer people actually have official letterhead.) What I mean is, put your logo or your record company's logo at the top of the page.

Your press release should be formatted like this:

1.   Top Line: **"FOR IMMEDIATE RELEASE"**

All press releases start with <u>FOR IMMEDIATE RELEASE</u> written in the top left hand corner, and always in CAPS and underlined.

2. The Contact Information

Contact Info should include your first and last name (or the first and last name of your contact person), a phone number and an e-mail address. The web address is optional here, or you can include it at the bottom in the additional contact information section.

The top of the Press Release should look like this:

FOR IMMEDIATE RELEASE
Contact: Ariel Hyatt (212) 239-8384
Contact@ArielPublicity.com

3. Headline

Next comes the headline of the press release, which should be simple, centered, and bold. An example:

Jen Chapin to Celebrate Release of New Album
with East Coast Tour

4. Subhead

This is an expanded part of the headline, which brings the reader in and accentuates the headline by adding detail.

An example:

The daughter of the late great Harry Chapin is heading out on a 10-city tour to support Ready, *her new album on Metropolitan Hybrid.*

Tour stops will Include Philadelphia, Boston, Portland, and Hartford.

5. Opening Paragraph: **Location, Date, & 5Ws**

The opening paragraph should start with *(City, State)
Date*—This is so the reader knows where the information is coming from and how timely the information is.

Example: *(New York, NY) June 20, 2012*

And it should answer the 5W's: *Who, What, When,
Where* and *Why.*

This initial paragraph should always grab the reader and answer all of the basic questions the reader might have. These are factual. If the release is to promote a show or a specific event, include the full date, venue name, venue address, show time, ticket price, and ages as well as a link to the venue for further directions and information.

6. Second Paragraph: **USP (Unique Selling Point) /Quotes**

This is the "meat" of your press release, so make
it juicy!

This will include further information, more details, an engaging story, a quote about your music or about the topic of the release from reviewers, fans, a producer, a venue owner or an industry tastemaker (because what other people say is always taken more seriously and is more believable than your own hype). Your "pitch" from "Week 2" should also be included here. (Pretend that the reader may never actually hear the CD.)

7. Final Details **& Additional Contact Information**

Here is where you would include all tour dates, a mailing address, a link to your websites, and a place where a photo can be downloaded. A link where the CD or tracks can be purchased and a label contact can also be added here.

8. THE 3 # # #'S—THE END!

Now type this: ###

This indicates that the press release is finished and there is not another page.

How to Be Your Own Publicist: A Step-By-Step Guide To Garnering Maximum Attention

The first article I ever wrote back in the late '90s that has since been re-published many places, including online at *The Indie Bible, ColoradoMusic.org, Womanrock* and in print at *Nightflying.* And since then, many artists have come up to me at conferences, called and e-mailed to say thanks for writing that article: "I followed what you said and I got results!" It's been updated every year since and here it is:

Intro—The State of Music Publicity Now

Music publicity has changed radically in the past few years. Here are the days of *Pro Tools,* cheap CD manufacturing (or DIY at home with a color printer) and the Internet—immediate access to the release and distribution of free music and total information overload at the tip of your fingers!

There are more bands on the road than ever before—there are thousands of brand-new releases each and every week—and fewer and fewer traditional media outlets writing about new music. This combination, from a traditional publicist's perspective, is lethal. However, it is still possible for an indie artist to get attention.

Publicity, like building a fan base, takes time, dedication and effort. When you are doing a PR campaign the effort is usually Herculean compared to the result. (If you gauge the result solely on how many articles get written.)

Publicity is time consuming and detail oriented. But with a bit of planning and focus, you can spin your own publicity wheel—all it takes is foresight, organization and patience.

The artist who plans well and understands publicity is the artist who receives the most PR. The good news is that the publicity process for any band, no matter how big or small, is very much the same. Of course, the size of the publications in which you place articles can vary dramatically. (This is based on what style of music is hot at the moment, combined with record sales, label status and your "newsworthiness.")

For this article, I interviewed two music journalists. Their comments and advice are included throughout. I also included several web links to help you along. The two writers I have quoted here are:

> **Kristi Singer**—Writes for: *American Songwriter, Singer & Musician Magazine, Sun News* and *The Wilmington Star News*, among others.

Waleed Rashidi—Writes for: *Alternative Press, Modern Drummer, Alarm, MeanStreet, Law of Inertia,* and *e-online,* among others.

It was fun to interview writers who usually interview my artists. It provided a lot of insight to get their opinions on what they like to see from bands...as well as what they don't.

PART ONE—The Printed Press Kit

A printed press kit is a critical component to add when sending out your CD to anyone in the industry who needs to understand the details and background information on you. Your press kit that goes out to journalists should vary slightly from the one you send out to get gigs. (This one should include all four elements listed on the next page PLUS past touring history in detail, as well as your stage plot.)

> MYTH: I don't need a press kit—people can see all of my information on my website.
> TRUTH: Your press kit *is* still a vital and important component to your overall marketing strategy.

Writers are very busy people who are constantly under deadline, so don't EVER make a writer work to get information about your band. Press kits help them access information quickly and efficiently. A big, fat press kit in a folder won't impress. Writers will only become exasperated by a press kit that is not succinct and to the point.

The 4 Steps:

The first step in your journey is to create a press kit, which consists of four steps / components:

1. The bio
2. The photo / images
3. Articles, quotes and CD reviews
4. The CD

STEP 1: The Bio

Create a one-page bio that is succinct and interesting to read. I strongly advise hiring a bio writer if you can afford one.

If you are not ready to pony up the cash, enlist an outside source to help you out. I find that people who are great storytellers make great bio writers.

TIP: Many music journalists write bios as well as articles, so if you read a great profile on a band in a local paper, on a blog, or in a music magazine, don't hesitate: Track that writer down and ask him if he writes band / artist bios.

> *Waleed:* "A bio does not have to be extensive. I want a general idea of the band's history and some key shows (but please, not a whole show history). I love the "recommended if you like" line. I know some artists hate to compare themselves to others but I definitely like that; it makes the sorting process easier."

Include your Pitch towards the top of the page. Create an introduction that sums up your sound, style and attitude in a few brief sentences. This way, if a writer is pressed for time, he can simply take a sentence or two from your bio and place it directly in the publication. If you try to make a writer dig deeply for the gist, that writer will most likely put your press kit aside and look to one of the other 30 press kits that arrived that week.

Avoid vague clichés such as "melodic," "brilliant harmonies," "masterful guitar playing," "tight rhythm section," etc. These are terms that can be used to describe any artist and music.

TIP: Try to create a bio with the assumption that the vast majority of music writers may never get around to listening to your music. Also, writers are usually under tight deadlines to produce copy, so many CDs and MP3s fall by the wayside. But that doesn't mean that you can't get a great calendar pick or photo inclusion.

STEP 2: The Photo

It is very tough to create a great band photo. In the thousands I have encountered, only a few have had creativity and depth. It is vital to arrange a photo shoot, and you have to take this seriously. You will benefit from it in the long run.

Create a photo that is clear, light, and attention grabbing. Five musicians sitting on a couch or standing against a brick wall is not interesting. If you have a friend who knows how to use photo editing tools, I recommend you enroll him to help you do some funky editing to really make it pop.

MYTH: We need to have 8" x 10" photos.

TRUTH: Gone are the days of the 8" x 10". Color postcards or printed images on your bio with links will suffice. And publications will download the photos they will run directly from your website.

My company recommends printing 3" x 5" or 4" x 6" double-sided 4-color postcards. They look great and very professional. And any extra postcards that are not used in press kits can be sent to people on your mailing list, or you can give them away at gigs.

You must make sure your photo is easily downloadable in hi res (300 dpi) on your website so journalists who want images can get them easily. Make sure that the jpg appears PROPERLY LABELED after it is downloaded, with your name and the names of band members from left to right.

I suggest putting several color images, both vertical and horizontal, in your online press kit, so editors can choose which ones they like best and which work for their layout. Include your album cover for download as well, so if they run an album review, they can have the artwork to go with it.

Postcards or dropcards should have an image of the band on one side and an image of your album cover with the URL of your website on the other side. You can also include the release date of your upcoming album, your contact numbers, and your pitch or a quote about your sound from the media.

There are many great inexpensive printers available online. We order our postcards from the following two sources:

http://www.jakprints.com
http://www.1800postcards.com

You can also use dropcards as a great alternative.

> **Waleed:** "The best types of photos are ones that are crop-able in a vertical or horizontal format; sometimes when I have to fill a hole in the magazine I may need a photo that will fit it into any frame. I also like photos that have room around the photo; this way I can put text around the photo. I want a photo that depicts a band in the way they are. A junkie band should be in a junkyard, a clean band should be in a cleaner atmosphere; environment, wardrobe and location are all very important, as is creativity. I get overkill of fisheye lenses and overkill on oversaturated colors. Try not to copy too much of what is going on."

TIP: Don't make journalists hunt around for the photos—they will not go to someone else's site to grab them. Downloadable color photos should be readily available on your website, and should be at least 300 dpi and easily findable and downloadable with less than 3 clicks.

Put the band members' names from left to right (l-r) under the band photo to give journalists a point of reference. (Many publications publish photos with all band members' names from left to right to save the writers the trouble of having to ask for the names.)

STEP 3: The Articles, Quotes, and CD Reviews

Getting that first article written about you can feel daunting. Two great places to start are your local hometown papers (assuming that you don't live in NYC, Chicago, or Los Angeles) and any music website that you like.

TIP: You can archive additional articles on your website, and if a writer wants to read more than that, he can visit your site for further information. If you don't have anything written about you yet, not to worry—this will soon change.

TIP: Use Google, Twitter, and Facebook as resources to find reviewers you want to contact, or work backwards and search for indie bands that you would be compared to and see who has written about them.

Call or e-mail the reviewers that wrote about them, politely introduce yourself, and ask if you can send them your CD, or your SoundCloud or Bandcamp links for consideration. This is a much better technique than the old-school method of getting a "media list" and blindly mailing precious materials out in bulk.

Always Follow Up—75% of Musicians Never Do

> *Kristi:* "Seventy-five percent of all bands don't follow up with me aggressively enough. I often am on deadline and I will ask a band to call me back in a week, and most never do."

"I keep new CDs in 3 piles in my office:

1. The pile I am about to write about because they have assigned.

2. The pile I really want to pitch to my editors because I think they will like it or because it fits the publication.

3. The pile that I have no idea what they are, and no one followed up with me on them, so I never get to them.

There could be some wonderful and appropriate CDs sitting in my office that I could write about, but if no one pitched me on them they usually get overlooked."

Waleed: "I think it is important to follow up on all mailings. Seventy-five to eighty percent of indie bands that send me stuff never follow up, and those CDs always fall through the cracks."

STEP 4: **The CD**

The CD artwork, like the press kit, must be well thought out. You should customize your press kit so that it looks in sync with your CD. This way, when a writer opens up a package the press kit and the CD look like they go together. Do not bother sending out advance burns of your CD unless the writer requests them. Full artwork is always preferred.

Kristi: "I enjoy getting full artwork CDs. Advances and burned CDs are not as intriguing. Presentation is very important."

Waleed: "My micro pet peeve is that I do not like CDs that do not have jewel cases (or at least spines). If a CD is in a baggie or a thin sleeve it makes the CD impossible to find."

A few months ago the "PR List" (a group of music publicists—over 600 of us) ran a survey of music journalists asking them if they would take downloads over CDs. The overwhelming response was: ***Send me the full CD with artwork or don't send anything at all.***

So, for journalists, send the full CD with color artwork and most importantly a **readable spine,** so your CD can be found amongst the piles when you call to follow up.

TIP: Put your phone number and contact info in the CD, so if it gets separated from the press kit, the writer knows how to contact you. Also, "Recommended Tracks" stickers are great for the press (suggesting no more than 2 or 3 selections).

TIP: Don't waste precious CDs. That means only send a CD if you are sure a writer actually writes CD reviews (few newspaper writers are given the space to run them these days, so check first).

> ***Waleed:*** "I like well-organized packages as well that are stapled together, so I can take a minute to get through it and flip through cohesive info. And PLEASE put contact info EVERYWHERE—on the CD, on the bio and on the photo."

PART 2—Getting the Word Out

Internet—Getting Your Online Press Materials Together

First, duplicate your finished press kit electronically. Either make a PDF of it that you can send to writers as attachments or open an account with SonicBids or ReverbNation and drop all of your information into an EPK.

http://www.sonicbids.com

http://bit.ly/ReverbPK

Your Website

If you don't already have an updated website that you are proud to show off to the world, get one ASAP! Register a memorable name and remember: .com is much easier than .net or .org.

Tour Press—Getting Your Press Materials Out

Start planning PR for any tour 6-8 weeks before you hit the road. As soon as a gig is booked, ask the promoter for the club's press list (most clubs have one). Promoters are dependent on this local press to help sell tickets.

Have the press list e-mailed to you and reach out to the appropriate journalists on it. Don't be shy: You are working with the promoter to make the show happen, and promoters love it when the show is well publicized.

TIP: Ask the promoter which writers like to receive CDs for review vs. which ones are okay with downloading music. Also be sure to ask the promoter who his favorite writers are and which ones will like your style of music.

> *Kristi:* "I really enjoy it when the band adds a personal note with their press kit. A short and sweet note is that extra personal touch that really makes a huge difference."

TIP: If the local promoter has a publicist, let that publicist do her (or his) job. Pack up everything and mail it to the promoter's publicist, or send him all the links he will need to send to the media. This publicist knows the writers in his or her hometown and will be instrumental in helping you.

Don't get territorial about your PR! You should allow anyone who is willing to help to do so.

Locating Publications

If the club does not have a press list, you can easily search Google for a good target list.

TIP: With monthly publications, if you are not at least 8 weeks out, don't bother sending to them.

Work Your Niche Angles

Work any angles you may have. Is the lead singer in the band Jewish or Irish? Is someone in the band a parent? Most major markets have a Jewish publication, an Irish publication, and a parenting magazine. And these are great angles to work.

TIP: Many smaller local publications only cover events and people from certain areas, so if someone in the band is from the town where you are touring, make sure you let the local editors know.

Following Up Is Critical

It is critical that you follow up. As you read in Part 1 of this article, 75% of all indie bands never follow up and writers do not include bands that they don't know if they do not hear from them. When you call the writers, understand that you will be leaving messages 90% of the time.

Leave short and sweet messages that include your phone number and e-mail address as well as your show date and venue to spark the writer's memory. 9 times out of 10, writers will not call you back; that's okay, because you have given them everything they will need.

If you do get them on the phone, don't be afraid to say which promoter recommended you, and always invite them to the show. Don't let all that voice-mail discourage you. I have placed hundreds of articles, mentions, and photos without ever speaking to the writer.

> **Waleed:** "The one piece of advice I would give an indie artist is: Be tactful about your pitches and be mindful that writers have to listen to you as well as thousands of other bands in any given month. But also don't be afraid to reach out. It is a journalist's job to listen to new music. Don't give up, but at the same time don't bombard; be mindful not only about your career but also about their careers as well."

Persevere

The first few times you play a market, you may not get any press. If you are totally new to the scene and are worried because a paper did not cover you the first time around, keep sending that paper information every time you play in the area. I have never met a writer who ignores several press kits from the same artist sent over and over again.

Have Patience

PR is a slow-moving vehicle that can take time to get results. I have worked with some bands that needed to go through a market three or four times before any results started showing up in the press.

When you send materials on repeated occasions, include a refresher blurb to remind the writer of your style. Always include the following information: date, show time, ages, ticket price, club name and address, and who is on the bill. Don't make writers hunt around for event info. Make their job as easy as possible by providing all the information.

Also keep in mind that some writers will probably not write about you over and over again. If you hit the same markets continually, a great tactic is to change your photo every few months.

Bonus Round—More Marketing Elements

Posters

Posters are a great form of PR and they don't have to cost you a fortune. I highly recommend 4-color posters, and it's a good idea to create a space on the bottom where you or the promoter can fill in the show info.

The most cost-effective way to make posters is to buy 11" x 17" colored paper from your local paper store (comes in reams of 500) and run off copies at the copy shop. Make several copies on white paper and include these with your colored posters; this way the promoter can make extras, if needed.

TIP: Make sure you ask the promoters how many posters they would like and send them along with the press kits. After a few days, it's best to call and verify that the posters and press materials were received and are hanging up in the venue.

Your Street Team—Virtual or Real World

Enroll your biggest fan to be the head of your street team. Put this person in charge of reaching out to other fans who will join the street team in each market you visit.

In exchange for a few tickets to your show, some merch, and some love from you, your field staff will put up posters and talk to their college newspaper about writing a feature or the local radio station about spinning your CD.

If you are not playing out, that's okay; they can help you manage your online portals, and hit all social networking sites to get the word out about you and your music.

TIP: Street Team Management: To get a street team started, include a sign-up column on your mailing list and a form to fill out on your website. Manage your street team using the FREE tools at:
http://bit.ly/ReverbStreetTeam

WRITTEN EXERCISE: ANALYSIS OF YOUR OWN PRESS KIT

(Note: If you do not have a press kit yet, you can skip this one!)

Nothing is more effective in making improvements than taking a step back and reassessing. A few times a year you should take yourself through this exercise in order to make your presentation as good as it can be.

For this exercise, pull out your press kit—either the physical version, or the one on your website.

Bio Re-Vamp:

Read over your bio and write down the following things in your journal:

1. Is the overall tone of your bio an interesting and captivating story, or is it a résumé of things that you have done? (If your answer is "résumé," it's time for a re-write!)

2. Where does your bio first take your reader?

3. Does the introduction (the first few lines) bring the reader in?

    › Is it interesting, or does it use classic band mistake words such as "unique," "melodic," etc.? or "the (name of band) started playing music together in 2001"?

BORING!!

1. Are there other clichés you could avoid, like explaining each song on the album and what it means, etc.? (Keep in mind the reader possibly has not listened to any of your music.) Circle the clichés or write them here.

2. Is your pitch located somewhere within the first few lines of your bio so people can get an immediate hit of what you are all about? Re-write the beginning of your bio to include a sentence that draws in the reader and contains your pitch so that the reader becomes instantly engaged.

3. What is the most interesting thing about you/your band as a **story**?

4. Would this bio be captivating to people who have never met you—if not, is there a missing aspect that you could add to make it more enticing?

5. **Now, go beyond your bio:** Aside from bio editing, what aspects of your overall press kit could you improve?

For example:

> Design Layout /Format/Type Style/Graphic Elements/Photos
> Stories/Testimonials
> Stronger Press Quotes
> Niche Angles

Are all these elements as good as they could be?

TIP: If you need press quotes, ReviewYou can link you to great bloggers for CD reviews guaranteed in two weeks: *http://www.reviewyou.com*

WRITTEN EXERCISE: GETTING QUOTES TO ADD TO YOUR PRESS KIT

Here's an exercise to help you identify people who you can ask for some quotes to include in your press kit.

Part 1: Fans

Write down the names of your 5 most enthusiastic fans.

1.

2.

3.

4.

5.

Part 2: The Music Industry

Write down the answers to the following questions.

1. Who books you at clubs?

2. Who produced, mixed or mastered your album?

3. Do you have any friends in bands a bit further along than you who could give you a quote?

4. Do you know members of the media or Radio DJs? (Don't worry if they have actually written about you. You don't have to have been covered by someone to get a quote from that writer.)

5. Are there any blogs, websites or other publications that have covered you?

Part 3: How to Ask

This part is easy!

People *love* to be quoted because it's more publicity for them, so just concoct a simple e-mail asking if they wouldn't mind providing a quote.

Here is an example of an e-mail I use:

> *Subject Line of E-mail:*
> **Fishing For Compliments...**
>
> *Dear Joe,*
>
> *I am updating my website by gathering quotes to add to the testimonials section of my site.*
>
> *I would love a quote from you (which I will of course credit you for with a link back to your website).*
>
> *Might I be so bold as to ask for a quote about your experience working with us (or coming to our shows)?*
>
> *Thanks, Ariel*

Traditional PR Part 2—A Musician's Guide to Choosing Tthe Perfect Publicist

Here is my guide to choosing a publicist.

I wrote this to help you navigate the ever-expanding world of music PR and offerings in the marketplace, and to help you avoid many of the costly pitfalls my clients have fallen into before they worked with my company. I just got a call recently from a veteran musician who did his homework and avoided hiring one firm with a horrible reputation—only to get all of his money taken by another publicist whose phone was disconnected the day after the check cleared.

I'm not saying this is commonplace in the industry. There are numerous wonderful publicists working hard as you read this, and I have designed this guide as a service to you, so that you can choose the perfect publicist that is just right for you and your team. I totally understand that we were not born with the innate knowledge of what PR is, or how it differs from advertising and other types of promotion you may be looking into—in fact, my first day as an intern at a fancy public relations firm, I asked my supervisor, "What is PR, exactly?" He looked at me like I had 10 heads and said, "PR is, well... it's PR!" Hmmm... okay, glad we got that straight, I thought to myself.

Read on to find out more.

6 Major Benefits of Hiring A Great Publicist

There are a lot of good reasons for hiring a wonderful publicist to add to your team.

(I use "she" a lot when referring to publicists because the vast majority are women, no offense to the men in my field.)

1. A publicist can make you look great on paper with a fabulous bio written by a professional. She can also strategize and create a story about you that you may have never thought up.

2. She can help you hone your pitch so you can sell yourself whenever you are talking to anyone.

3. She will increase your name awareness.

4. If you are a touring artist, she can get you tour press in all the local markets where you are scheduled to play.

5. She can get you legitimate press quotes to add to your arsenal, which you can then show your potential team when hiring a radio promoter, retail rep, manager, label, and distribution company. You can also add these quotes to your website and to your press kit.

6. She will save you a ton of work by leveraging her contacts and relationships.

5 Common Misconceptions about Publicists & Publicity Campaigns

Here are some common misconceptions about publicists and publicity campaigns in general.

MISCONCEPTION #1: She Sounded Really Together and Ambitious on the Telephone. She Must Be Amazing!

Sometimes yes and sometimes no. A publicist's job is to sell on the telephone and many of them will naturally do a great job of selling themselves to you. Unfortunately, there are a few publicists that have reputations for not delivering great work (or even one single report) after they take your money. So it is critical that you do your research.

MISCONCEPTION #2: If I Hire a Publicist, She Can Create Magical Opportunities!

Nope. She can't work miracles, but she can introduce you to the media and help you once you have a defined strategy and a roadmap. Hiring a publicist is just the beginning of your work. You need to keep her busy with stories and angles and events to work throughout her time managing your campaign. A publicist is only as good as whatever she is publicizing, and it is critical to give her as much to use as possible.

MISCONCEPTION #3: She Works For a Huge Band; She Knows All These People; She Will Get Me in *Rolling Stone*!

NO! Publicists should absolutely be hired for who they know and other clients they represent. And their relationships at national publications are critical. But be warned: Larger bands, on major labels, with big followings and scalable sales numbers, get articles over smaller, up-and-coming artists a lot of the time. If you are an emerging artist, you sometimes need to build up to the larger publications.

This does not mean that the publicist should not try to get you placement; she should. Just know that even the tightest personal relationships don't equal articles. Of course, the publicist knows these people and can always ask, but it is absolutely not a guarantee that you're going to get articles written about you. So, you must always strategize about what your angle is before you get into it. And, while national PR is possible for all artists at all levels, it must be appropriately handled. An artist with no national distribution and minimal sales is not likely to end up on the pages of *Rolling Stone* or *Spin* unless there is a fabulous story around the band that needs to be told to an international audience.

MISCONCEPTION #4: I'm Gonna Be On National TV!

Television shows such as *Late Night*, *Ellen*, and even *The Tonight Show* do showcase independent artists from time to time. But not all publicists have the connections to get you on these TV shows. In order to avoid a major letdown, discuss this with your publicist before you hire her. You can ask: "Have you ever placed anyone on national TV?" And: "How many artists have played and on which shows?" She will be honest both in her ability to reach the bookers and about what chances she thinks you may have to actually end up on one of these shows.

MISCONCEPTION #5: If I Hire A Publicist, Hundreds Of Articles Will Be Written About Me!

Nope. It is critical to manage your own expectations. I'm not saying, "Aim low." But you must have more than a very compelling story (and of course great music) for anyone to write about you; you must also have a reason to receive media coverage. Just having an album release or a couple of local shows is not actually grounds for national coverage and many larger publications may pass you up the first campaign around. That's okay; this should be considered a building block and not a rejection. Of course playing the numbers does help. So the more appropriate journalists your publicist reaches out to and sends your music to, the better the chances of placements.

9 Critical Things You Should Know About Publicity Before You Make Your First Move

I talk to musicians all day who call looking to hire a publicist, and I've noticed that many artists don't really understand what publicity is. The following list will clarify the concept of publicity for you.

1. The Definition of Publicity.

First, we are going to start out with the very basics— some definitions of what publicity is exactly, according to the Merriam-Webster Dictionary:

Publicity

"An act or device designed to attract public inter-
est; specifically: information with news value
issued as a means of gaining public attention or
support. Also: The dissemination of information
or promotional material."

I couldn't have said it better myself. Publicity is exactly
these things.

A music publicist is hired as a member of your team to
represent you to the media. Media is defined tradition-
ally as editors and writers at newspapers, magazines,
college journals, and television. Some publicists may
also cover radio for interviews on tour stops. But if you
want to get on the radio charts (like CMJ), you will need
a radio promoter. More and more publicists also cover
Internet PR, like my company. But not all traditional
publicists do this, so make sure to ask before you hire.

A publicist's job is to liaise with the press. They are not
hired to get you a booking agent or gig, a label deal, a
distribution deal, or any other type of marketing deal.
That is what a manager is for. A well-connected publicist may be able to hook you up with all of the above-
mentioned things, but it is not in her job description.

2. You Are in the Driver's Seat.

Remember, as the artist, you are the buyer here, and
you are shopping for PR. You are in the driver's seat.
It's your money and your music that keep publicists in
business. Hiring a publicist is like hiring another guitar
player for your band. Choose one you like, who fits your

vision and your goals. All too many times I've heard that a publicist was hired in spite of the artist's personal opinions. You should like your publicist, and she should be the right one for you.

3. With Publicity, You Pay for Effort—Never for Results.

I have had disgruntled artists call me and say, "I hired a publicist and I only got six articles. That cost me $1,000 per article!" Sadly, this is not how you quantify a PR campaign. How you quantify a PR campaign is by how many albums were sent out and what the responses were, even if they were inconclusive or negative. You pay for the amount of effort the publicist made on your behalf. Of course, you should get some and even many results. Getting nothing is totally unacceptable. But you never know when your publicist's efforts will show up months, and sometimes years, after your campaign is complete.

4. A PR Campaign Needs to Be Planned Well in Advance.

For long-lead press (that means magazines with national distribution like *Spin* and *Rolling Stone*), the editors put their publications to bed three full months before they hit the newsstands. So if your CD is coming out in October, you must have it pressed with full artwork and ready with materials to mail in July. Of course not all PR campaigns focus on national press, but no publicist will take you on with zero lead-time, so you definitely need to prepare lead-time in every case.

193

Recommended Publicity Campaign Lead Times:

» **National Campaign**—3-4 months before the release

» **Tour Press Campaign**—4-6 weeks before the shows

» **Local Campaign**—4-6 weeks before placement

» **Online Campaign**—2-3 weeks before placement (*minimum*)

(Placement = article, CD review, calendar listing, TV/radio interview, etc.)

5. The 4 Components of a Press Kit.

A good press kit consists of 4 parts: the bio; the photo; the articles, quotes & CD reviews; the CD.

The Bio—Create a one-page bio that is succinct and interesting to read. I strongly advise hiring a bio writer (this should cost between $200-$400). If you are not ready to pony up the cash, enlist an outside source to help you. I find people who are great storytellers make great bio writers.

The Photo—Arrange a photo shoot; if you take this seriously, you will benefit deeply. Create a photo that is clear, light, and attention-grabbing. Showing movement is a plus (sitting on a couch or up against a brick wall is not interesting). If you have a friend who knows how to use PhotoShop, enroll him to help you do some funky and fun editing.

The Articles, Quotes & CD Reviews—Getting that first article written about you can feel daunting. Two great places to start are your local hometown papers (assuming you don't live in NYC or Los Angeles), and any music websites or blogs you like.

The CD—The CD artwork, like the press kit, must be well thought out. Do not bother sending out advance burns of your CD unless the writer requests them. Full artwork is always preferred. Put your phone number and contact info in the CD so if it gets separated from the press kit, the writer knows how to contact you.

6. Publicity is a Marathon, Not a Sprint.

PR is very different in nature from a radio campaign that has a specific ad date and a chart that you are paying to try to get listed on. There is no Top 40 publicity chart. With the sheer number of albums coming out into the marketplace (approx 1,000 per week), it could take months longer than your publicity campaign runs to see results.

7. Online Publicity is Just as Important as Offline Publicity.

I would argue that online PR is *more* important, because today's newspaper is tomorrow's recycling. Online publicity goes up fast, and it can be around for months and sometimes for years.

Current research—and sales figures—show that people are reading newspapers less and less with every passing day. More people rely on the Internet as their main news source, and on recommendations from friends, so Internet placements are absolutely wonderful and totally legit, and they can help your Google rankings as well.

8. Publicity Does Not Sell Records.

If you are hiring a publicist to see a spike in your CD sales, I have news for you: There is absolutely no correlation between getting great PR and selling records.

PR is designed to raise awareness of you in the press, to help build a story, and also build up critical acclaim—and, of course, a great article can lead to sales. But overall, if selling albums is your goal, PR is not the only thing you will need to reach it; you will also need to build your loyal fan base and take care of fans with sweet offers.

9. All Publicity is Good Publicity.

I know we have all heard this, but it's a great thing to really understand. If one of your goals in PR is to get your name out there (and this should be a goal), the truth is that the average person remembers very little of what they read. Only a tiny percentage gets retained. If you really think that readers are going to remember a tepid or a mediocre review of your album, the answer is, they won't.

And never ever take your own PR seriously. As my favorite artist Andy Warhol once said, "Don't read your press; weigh it."

Making Initial Contact: The 3 Questions to Ask Any Publicist First

I get a lot of complaints from artists who call me and say that they tried to get certain PR firms on the telephone, but that they never got a call back or that they had trouble getting them to respond at all. Speaking in defense of a busy PR firm, many of them are just too crazed with work to handle all of the incoming inquiries. However, with a little finesse you can get to them. This is not a guarantee that they will want to take you on as a client, but it will at least get you in the door.

Here is a simple 3-step system that will get you into a conversation with a busy PR firm, after you have done your research and decided which PR firms you would like to target.

But first, a note of precaution and a checklist.

Most major PR firms (the ones that have national acts on their rosters) have strict criteria for accepting clients, and many of them plan campaigns months in advance. So here is a checklist of what you need to have in place before the big firms will be interested:

1. National brick-and-mortar distribution—CD Baby or Tunecore may not be enough of a distribution plan for some larger PR firms who deal with national publications. (Please tell me the last time you read: "Available at CD Baby" in *Rolling Stone*.) I'm not saying you need to have national traditional distribution, because personally I don't think it's a great idea for most artists at this point. I'm just letting you know what PR firms sometimes require.

2. A release date that is at *least* 3-4 months away from your initial contact (preferably 5-6 months).

3. A tour in place or some kind of local or interesting angles to discuss.

STEP 1: **Pick up the Phone.**

Never wimpily e-mail a request to hire a PR firm, it makes you look unprofessional.

When you make initial contact with a public relations firm, don't just dive in and start firing questions at whoever answers the telephone. Note that a very busy intern or an administrative assistant may be in charge of answering the phones and that intern will not be able to tell you prices or PR firm availability, so know who you are talking to and know who to ask for.

TIP: Visit the "About Us" section of the PR firm's website and read the names of the people working at the firm, so you know who you may be either speaking to or asking for. And always ask for someone specific by name.

STEP 2: If You Are Asked to Leave a Message, Don't Take it Personally.

I can't tell you how busy a PR firm with a large roster of clients can be. You will be put into voice-mail or someone will take a message. DO NOT just leave your name and phone number!! Leave a full and concise message saying the following:

» **Your name**—first and last, your band name, and your URL.

» **Your telephone number**—just ONE number, not work, home and mobile.

» **Your reason for calling**—"I am interested in hiring a PR firm and I am inquiring about your availability."

If the person asks you for more detail then give it, but don't volunteer your release date and a lot of additional details. That is what the conversation with the appropriate person is for. If no one calls you back within 72 hours, call again and repeat. Three strikes and move on.

If a PR firm can't call you back after three tries, then they are not the firm for you.

STEP 3: When You Get the Publicist on the Phone …

It is highly probable that the publicist you want to speak to is under deadlines for the day, and you must respect that she has a job to do. So when you do get someone on the phone on first contact, ask only three questions.

But, first introduce yourself very briefly:

"Hi, I'm _____ and I'm in a rock band from Los Angeles about to release our new album."

And here are the three questions:

1. Are you considering new clients for the time frame of _____ (your release date)?

2. Give a very brief synopsis of your project, three sentences max. Include:

   › The genre of music you play.
   › Your proposed release date.
   › Your distribution plan. It's fine if the album is only digitally distributed or only available through CD Baby, but make sure you tell her that and know this may not be appropriate for her firm.
   › Your tour schedule, with markets and highlights.
   › Any other parts of your release plan, like your radio promotion, your retail promotions, your street teams that will be in place, etc.

3. The third question to ask is, "May I send you my music on CD or links to my tracks and set up a time to follow up?"

199

Is She Really That Good? 4 Research Tips to Help You Find Out

Tons of publicists can sound really together and ambitious on the telephone, and they should. This is their job. But, sadly, there are quite a few publicists that are known for not delivering great work or being accountable to their clients. So it is critical that you do some due diligence and research.

There are 4 ways we suggest that you research publicity firms.

1. Google Search the individual names of each publicist, and the name of the company, and look for information about these individuals.

2. Google Search the different bands and artists that the PR firm represents in Google news search and Google blog search, and check out where the placements (articles and stories) have happened. If you don't see a lot of articles on the artists this may not be a great sign.
   http://news.google.com
   http://blogs.google.com

3. Check out the CD Baby message boards. There is a lot of information about different publicists on the CD Baby boards, and clients from these PR firms have talked about their experiences. You can also post and ask for feedback here.
   http://cdbaby.org

4. Call the publicists' past clients, management, labels, and artists, and ask them what their experiences were.

How to Avoid 5 Costly PR Billing Rip Offs

When you decide to hire a publicist and she quotes you a price, that number usually represents the monthly retainer price. What I want you to be aware of is that on top of that monthly retainer there will be expenses, and you should always ask a simple question to avoid a surprise invoice after your first month onboard with your PR firm.

The simple question is:

> *"What do you bill for on top of your monthly retainer?"*

Here are the 5 common things that a PR firm will bill you for, and some advice on how to save some money. Before we went digital, I created over 1,000 traditional campaigns for artists, and many of them negotiated expenses before the campaign started. It is your right to do so.

#1—Telephone

A publicist's main tool is the telephone, and the truth is business landlines don't come cheap. A way of avoiding surprises is simply asking *"What is the average monthly charge for the telephone bill?"*

This is usually the same approximate number every month and the publicist will know it and quote you accordingly.

#2—Postage: Regular Mail, Fedex, and Messenger Services

Mail costs money; this we know. But ask your publicist if she charges a handling fee on top of regular first class postage. Many do, because they rent postage meters and pay fees for envelope stuffing, plus there is the cost of the labels, meter tape and ink. I know it sounds a little crazy, but until you own a postage meter I can't stress enough that the bloody thing is expensive to maintain!

$ MONEY SAVING TIP #1: Buy stamps, stuff your own envelopes, and send out your own initial mailer. This could save you hundreds of dollars if the PR firm is doing a large mailing on your behalf (over 100 envelopes). Invite your friends, open a bottle of vino and stuff away.

FedEx also costs money, and sometimes a writer is on a deadline and needs a CD the next day, so be prepared.

$ MONEY SAVING TIP #2: Be very aware that your publicist could be using "FedEx First," which costs $5 -$15 more to get it there first thing in the morning. So always have a conversation about what type of FedEx she uses and request "standard delivery" if that is possible.

Messenger services are a necessity and sometimes need to be used. Always ask what the charges are so you are not surprised. (It costs approximately $10 to deliver a small envelope in midtown Manhattan).

#3—Copies, Paper, and Envelopes

If your publicist is putting a press kit together for you, chances are she will be using paper and a copier. Ask how much she charges per page for copies.

$ MONEY SAVING TIP #3: Make the copies yourself at a local copy shop if it costs considerably less than your publicist charges. Drop them by her office by when she needs them, though you must respect her need to do her job with good lead-time. Padded envelopes are also very costly, so again, if it will save you a good amount of money, buy the envelopes and do the mailer yourself! Staples is NOT a great place to buy cheap padded mailers. For that, go here:

http://www.uline.com

#4—Burrelle's Clipping Service

Burrelle's is used by all major PR firms. Their job is to monitor every newspaper and magazine in the country (as well as radio, website and TV transcriptions), and when your name or your band's name shows up, they clip the article and mail the physical copy to your PR firm.

It's a wonderful service to have, and back in the day, before you could find a lot of content online, it was the only real way to monitor the success your publicist was having. But it is VERY expensive. Your publicist pays a high monthly retainer for it (approx. $500) plus about $2 per page per clip.

This means if you are mentioned on the cover of the entertainment section of the newspaper, then there is a photo and lead-in page and then an article on a third page, this can cost you $8. In addition, that article could be syndicated to many outlets and you will pay for copies of the same article (sometimes up to 20 or more).

With the Internet, it is not always necessary to have Burrelle's. But any top notch PR firm will have it and they will charge you for it.

$ MONEY SAVING TIP #4: Okay, this one won't get you the same amount of articles that Burrelle's will track because they RULE, but you can opt out of Burrelle's at your PR firm and sign up for Google Alerts and have Google track the articles that get placed.

http://www.google.com/alerts

You won't get the physical copies of each placement, but if you see an article you really love and need to have, you can always call the subscription department of each newspaper and order a copy for a few bucks.

#5—Gig Expenses: Transportation and Beverages

If your publicist and PR team come out to see you play a gig, they could easily bill you for their travel expenses such as cab / subway fare, or gas mileage. And if she brings a music writer to check you out, you could very well be buying that writer drinks at the bar.

So there you have it—the top 5 most frequent visitors on all of my clients' invoices.

$ MONEY SAVING TIP #5: Set a Pre-Negotiated Expenses Budget. You can say: I only want to spend $400 or $500 (or whatever number is comfortable for you) per month on expenses and ask your publicist to suggest ways to keep the number at this budget. That way, you will be completely prepared.

NOTES

CONCLUSION

Now that you have worked your way through these 9 Weeks, it is my sincerest hope that you have had a mental shift in your process and in your approach to your own marketing and PR.

As I said earlier in this book, this is a process, and the steps I've outlined can and should be visited over and over for long-term results.

I have hopefully added some tools to your arsenal that will help you over the long term, and I look forward to hearing about your results on the Mastermind Forum. Please do login and share with the community there.

If you ever need me you know how to find me, Twitter is best: *@CyberPR*. You can also keep in touch with me via my blog at *http://arielpublicity.com/blog*.

Here's to your success!

RESOURCES FOR FURTHER REFERENCE

20 Critical Websites for Musicians

Facebook, YouTube, and Twitter are not here. But that's because you are already using all 3 of these...right?

Here are 20 more sites you need to consider.

15-Second Pitch

15SecondPitch.com helps you craft, write, and fully define your 15-second elevator pitch. The pitch wizard on this site walks you through a step-by-step process to create it. The site also makes you more "Google-icious" because it ranks high in that mighty search engine.

Amazon

Amazon.com is a great place to create a profile that will be found in Google. On Amazon, you can curate lists of books, music, or products you really like as well as review albums and books you enjoy. You can also ask your fans to review your music on Amazon for more overall traction on the site.

Artist Data / Sonic Bids

Sonicbids.com is a great way to present your press kit and is a necessity if you want to submit to music festivals like SXSW and CMJ. The company now owns Artistdata.com, which helps you publish tour date information to a variety of destinations online from a single dashboard.

Bandzoogle

If you want a slick-looking website and don't want to pay a lot for it, I highly recommend *Bandzoogle.com*. They have many beautiful templates to fit your brand, and their customer support is wonderful.

Bit.ly

Bit.ly is a link-shortening site that helps you take long URLs that you may want to share with your community and makes them small (so you can fit them into tweets and Facebook status updates). And the best part is, it reports how many clicks and RTs you receive for each bit.ly you create.

Blogging Platforms

Wordpress, Blogger, and Tumblr are 3 fast and easy sites where you can set up a blog, choose a theme, and be off to the races blogging for free in less than 20 minutes. A web designer can incorporate all 3 of these sites easily into your own site.

Foursquare

If you swear by your mobile phone, you may love *Four-square.com*, a location-based social networking service. Foursquare enables you to "check-in" to the places you visit—bars, stores, restaurants, etc.—so you can keep track of where your friends are hanging out, and so they can find you too. You can collect points and badges from the venues you visit the most and even earn coupons from your local merchants. Foursquare is all the rage these days, as it facilitates real-life interaction (much like Facebook's check-in feature.

Fan Funding Platforms

Pledge Music, RocketHub, IndieGoGo, Kickstarter—Okay, I know these are actually 4 sites, not one. But fan funding is such an important aspect to a musician's career in the new music business, so I did not want to single out just one platform. Each has its differences. But all help you to raise money from your fans for whatever purpose you want to use it.

FanBridge

If you do not have a newsletter management system in place and you are not sending newsletters regularly and consistently, look into *FanBridge*. The interface is easy to use, and the analytics and articles are amazing. You can easily educate yourself on best practices and measure your results.

Flickr

Flickr.com is the best online photo management and sharing application in the world. It's easy to post photos here; you can even port them over to your Wordpress blog, social media sites, and website easily for multi-portal display.

HootSuite

Hootsuite.com is a Twitter management tool that helps you see tweets based on lists, keywords or hashtags. It will help you schedule tweets and manage multiple accounts elegantly.

Hype Machine

Hypem.com is an MP3 and music blog aggregator that scans over 4,500 blogs each day and shows you the most popular songs and posts about music on the web. On *hypem.com*, you can always search and discover something new, and, if you want to, get the attention of respected music bloggers. You should start reading (and commenting on) featured blogs from the hypem network.

Jango

Jango.com is an online radio service that functions like Pandora. (You can curate whichever type of station you would like to listen to.) However, Jango has a twist: You can buy spins on it and tell Jango which artists you would like to be played alongside in other users' playlists. Listeners have the opportunity to give you direct feedback and even share their e-mail addresses with you.

Last.fm

Last.fm is a wonderful Internet radio site where you can create a profile (or update one that friends and fans have already created for you), create your own *Last.fm* stations, and tune into personalized radio. "Scrobbling" a song means that when you listen to it, the name of the song is sent to Lst.fm and added to your music profile. Songs you listen to will also appear on your *Last.fm* profile page for others to see.

Music Alley from Mevio

Music.mevio.com is a podsafe music platform where podcast hosts and producers can download pre-cleared music to include on their shows. Create a profile, upload your music, and track in real time as podcasters include you on their shows. Don't forget to listen in and thank them for including you.

Music Think Tank / Hypebot

MusicThinkTank.com (MTT) is a group blog that brings together ideas and thoughts from tastemakers in the online music business. I am a frequent contributor, and so is Derek Sivers. MTT is run by *Hypebot.com*, which is a great resource for all news that is music industry related.

Nimbit

Nimbit.com is a suite of great tools that can help you do many things, including: send and monitor your e-mail newsletters; build an affordable Wordpress site; streamline your social media; establish a store to sell your music and merchandise from your Facebook Fan Page.

ReverbNation

ReverbNation.com is an amazing site designed to empower artists with marketing tools. The deep stats and information the site provides about your fan base will help you make decisions about where to market, tour, and grow your business. Use them for e-mail management and for my favorite widget for collecting e-mails in exchange for songs: *http://bit.ly/reverbfreebribe*

RootMusic

RootMusic.com is my favorite free app for adding music to your Facebook Fan Page. RootMusic not only allows a music player and "buy" links to be added, but it also lets you skin your Facebook page so the whole look and feel of it matches your branding and colors.

Twitpic / Yfrog

Twitpic.com and *Yfrog.com* both allow you to use your mobile phone to snap pictures and easily upload them to your Twitter account as links on your tweetstream. This will also show up on your Facebook if you have them connected.

The "New" Music Business Dictionary*

Useful Definitions You Need to Know
Ariel's Favorites, *Not in Alphabetical Order

Blog
A Blog is really just an informal website. Blog sites are online journals or diaries that are usually more personal and more subjective than a proper website.

Audio-Blog
An Audio-Blog is a Blog that includes music as well as text. Usually the text is a critique or commentary of the music. Audio-Blogs are becoming more and more embraced by the industry. *The Globe & Mail* recently ran an in-depth article on Audio-Blogs that makes a great point: "People who maintain music blogs for little glory and no pay want to share their feelings about music, and use MP3 files to make the exchange more vivid."

Blogosphere
The collective countless blogs on the web (think atmosphere). There are currently over 100 million blogs online.

Podcast
A podcast, at its core, is an audio file that is created along with some code that enables the file to be downloaded to your computer, where it can be streamed in a player or downloaded to a portable player. There are now thousands of free podcasts available online and at iTunes.

Internet Radio Station

Listening to radio broadcasts via the Internet using streaming techniques. The audio is played via a software media player or a browser plug-in that supports streaming audio formats such as those from RealNetworks and Microsoft. Internet radio may be streamed at the same time as live AM and FM broadcasts over the air, or it may be a recording of a previous broadcast. In the latter case, selecting the station again after it started will reset the stream to the beginning.

Podsafe

Podsafe is a term created in the podcasting community to refer to any work which, through its licensing, specifically allows the use of the work in podcasting, regardless of restrictions the same work might have in other realms (Wikipedia).

RSS

RSS stands for "Really Simple Syndication" and is a web feed format used to publish frequently updated content such as blog entries, news headlines, or podcasts. RSS solves a problem for people who regularly use the web. It allows you to stay informed easily by retrieving the latest content from the sites you are interested in. You save time by not needing to visit each site individually. You ensure your privacy by not needing to join each site's email newsletter. The number of sites offering RSS feeds is growing rapidly and includes big names.

Wiki

(from oreilly.net) A wiki is a website where users can add, remove, and edit every page using a web browser.

It's so terrifically easy for people to jump in and revise pages that wikis are becoming known as the tool of choice for large, multiple-participant projects.

RSS Reader / Feed Reader

RSS content can be read using software called a "feed reader" or an "aggregator" such as Google Reader. The user subscribes to a feed by entering the feed's link into the reader or by clicking an RSS icon in a browser that initiates the subscription process.

The Icon looks like this:

Click on it to subscribe to anything you want.

Tagging

A tag is a (relevant) keyword or term associated with or assigned to a piece of information (e.g. a picture, article, or video clip), thus describing the item. Tags are usually chosen informally and personally by the author/creator or the consumer of the item. Tags are typically used for resources such as computer files, web pages, digital images, and Internet bookmarks (both in social bookmarking services, and in the current generation of web browsers). (*Wikipedia*)

Keyword

A keyword is the term used for words included in a web page that would match words used by web surfers in finding that web page (via a search engine). Keywords can simply be words included in the body text of the document, or added to the header using meta tags to increase the number of keywords (your web designer can easily do this). Selecting keywords, that match your target audience's use of the web is a critical marketing tactic. (*definethat.com*)

About Ariel Hyatt

Ariel Hyatt is a thought leader in the digital PR world: the founder of a successful PR firm; international speaker & educator and the author of two books on social media and marketing for artists. Ariel's Cyber PR® process marks the intersection of social media with engaged behavior, PR, and online Marketing.

Ariel foresaw the impact the advent of the internet and social media would have on public relations long before her peers. Following her vision, Ariel dove into the world of Digital PR in 2003. Her efforts to realize the public relations potential of social media resulted in innovation. Ariel developed her platform, Cyber PR®, to automate much of the traditional PR process and maximize client placement with new media makers.

Ariel's message is so compelling she has been invited to speak at festivals and conferences in twelve countries, including SXSW, CMJ, ASCAP's I Create Music, The Future of Music, Canadian Music Week, APRA's Song Summit (Sydney), You Are In Control (Reykjavik), The ECMAs, NARAS, Grammy Camp, and The Taxi Road Rally.

Ariel proudly serves on the advisory boards of Sweet Relief Musicians Fund, SXSW Accelerator, SoundCtrl, The New Music Seminar. She is an obsessive world traveler, a total foodie, and a vintage lunchbox collector.

Ariel Hyatt is also the author of *Musician's Roadmap to Facebook & Twitter.*

Where to Find Ariel

Ariel Publicity & Cyber PR®
http://www.ArielPublicity.com

Music Success in 9 Weeks
http://www.MusicSuccessInNineWeeks.com

Ariel's 2x-Per-Month Sound Advice Newsletter delivered to you
http://www.soundadviceezine.com

Watch Sound Advice TV
http://www.YouTube.com/ArielPublicity

Cyber PR® For Authors
http://www.CyberPRBooks.com

Products Available from Cyber PR®

Music Success in 9 Weeks–

Book (or eBook)

A step-by-step guide that walks you through how to supercharge your publicity, build your fan base, and earn more money. This book breaks down exactly how to achieve these goals in a week-by-week syllabus with written exercises.

> *"You need to buy this book, now! It's the only one that directly answers: 'I've got great music, but now what?' Read it, and you'll be earning its value back ten-fold."*
>
> *-Derek Sivers*, **Founder, CD Baby**

Each book comes with a lifetime membership to Ariel's exclusive online closed Mastermind Forum where you can join the community of artists working with the book and being coached by Ariel and her team. *http://www.MusicSuccessInNineWeeks.com*

Review You

A guaranteed CD review, written by a professional music blogger, delivered to you within 14 days. *Review You* covers all genres of music.

> *"I tried for months to get my CD reviewed. I read everything I could find on the subject and used their suggestions to the letter. After 20 mailings I received one review back—about three months later! There are so many of us out there that*

it's become increasingly harder to get our material reviewed. Thank God for ReviewYou.com!! The review I received from their staff writer was fantastic and gave me a lot to think about—and it was done in two weeks! This is a service that I will use over & over again."

-Paul Rader, **Independent Solo Artist**

Order your review now at: *http://www.reviewyou.com*

Musician's Roadmap to Facebook and Twitter

Your Complete Guide To Getting Liked, Followed & Heard

This book is loaded with graphics and multiple screen shots that clearly illustrate step-by-step everything from creating groups on Facebook to effective application installations to maximize your Facebook & Twitter profiles. Highlights include: Ariel's content strategies to help you diversify and become "sticky" to audiences online, Facebook vs. Facebook Fan Pages: Key differences you need to know; proven techniques that work for growing your fans and engagement on Facebook; and best applications for streaming & sharing music on Facebook and Twitter.

http://arielpublicity.com/musiciansroadmap

"Ariel has been helping bands navigate the digital ecosystem for as long as the ecosystem has existed and has built an extensive understanding of promotion on the leading online platforms. I can't think of a better person to help artists capture the

221

maximum value from the extraordinary potential that Twitter and Facebook offers."

- Brenden Mulligan, **Founder, ArtistData & Onesheet**

Cyber PR® Campaigns

Cyber PR® Gets Your Music Featured on Blogs, Podcasts, Internet Radio Stations, and More.

Ariel's firm represents musicians of all genres and from all over the world. Visit our website or call the office to find out how we can get your music into the hands of thousands of online social media makers.

http://www.cyberprmusic.com

(212) 239-8384

> *"Hiring Ariel Publicity was by far and in large the best money my band ever spent. Ariel starts right away and within days we had more publicity than our record label's publicity company had gotten us since we signed...worth every penny."*
>
> *~ Jeffrey Todd*, **Fort Pastor**

> *"Ariel has incomparable reach. Less than one month into my campaign, I've already been played around the world, in Australia, England, the US, the Netherlands, and more. I've already come across in-depth reviews of my debut album from widely-distributed bloggers to which I would otherwise have no contact. No effort is wasted, and I can follow the campaign, in detail, in real time. It's incredible, and it's working."*
>
> *~ Trey Green*

More Useful Web Definitions (This Time in Alphabetical Order)

Avatar

The graphic representation of a person online. It is typically used to help the person navigate a virtual world. Some try to make their avatars look like themselves, and others go for idealized/stylized visions.

Cloud Computing

Cloud computing is a service rather than a tangible product, and it is the process by which shared resources, software, and information are provided to computers and other devices over a network (the Internet). Examples include Google Docs and Spotify.

Folksonomy

A group of people working together to organize information into categories.

HTML:

This term stands for "Hyper Text Markup Language." It is a language used to develop and create web pages.

Hyperlink:

A graphic or word that opens another document when you click on it. Hyperlinks are the main way to navigate between different websites and between individual pages within one website.

Mashup:

A web service / software tool that joins two or more tools in order to create a whole new service. The term is also used to describe user-generated remixes of content from multiple sources.

Newsgroup:
A virtual area online reserved for the discussion of a particular topic.

Newsreader:
This service gathers the news from multiple blogs or news sites via RSS so that readers can access news from a single website or program. Online newsreaders (like Bloglines, Pluck, or Newsgator) are websites that allow you to read RSS feeds from within your web browser.

Opt In:
A direct, voluntary request by an individual e-mail recipient to have their email address added to a specific mailing list.

Opt Out:
An e-mail subscription practice that allows users that request it to be deleted from an e-mail distribution list by either selecting a link or sending an e-mail that requests their address be deleted.

Server:
A computer that houses websites and is connected to the Internet 24-hours per day.

Social Bookmarking:
The ability to save and categorize a personal collection of Internet bookmarks and share them with others. Users can also take bookmarks saved by others and add them to their own collection or subscribe to others' lists.

Social Media:

Online technologies that people use to share opinions, experiences, insights, and perspectives with each other.

Social Networking:

Websites that make it possible for people to link to others to share opinions, insights experiences and perspectives. The people sharing these ideas might be music fans on Twitter, business contacts on LinkedIn, classmates on Facebook, etc. Many media sites have now incorporated social networking features such as blogs, message boards, podcasts, and wikis to help build online communities related to their content.

Streaming Media:

Video or audio transmitted over a network that plays immediately when users click on it, without the need for a file download. RealMedia, QuickTime, and Windows Media are the most common streaming formats.

Tags:

Keywords attached to photos or web pages to help identify them and allow them to be logged by Google and other search engines.

URL:

This term stands for "Uniform Resource Locator." It is a string that supplies the Internet address of a website or page on the Internet.

Viral Marketing:

Any marketing technique that gets websites or users to pass on a marketing message to others.

Viral Video:
Video content, usually humorous in nature, that has become popular by sharing, usually via e-mail or media sharing websites.

Vlog:
Video-based journals that are posted online.

Web 3.0:
The evolution of web usage and interaction along several separate paths. The process by which the web has been transformed into a database as well as its movement towards making content accessible by multiple non-browser applications.

Webcasting:
Communicating to multiple computers at the same time over internet by "streaming" live audio and/or live video.

Webisode:
A short video that can only be found on the web.

Widget:
A third-party item that can be embedded in a web page.

Wiki:
A website or similar online resource that allows users to add and edit content collaboratively.

NOTES

CPSIA information can be obtained at www.ICGtesting.com
Printed in the USA
BVOW041629160112

280500BV00004B/4/P